ME
TOO

ME
TOO

EXTRAORDINARY,
EVERYDAY STORIES THAT CONNECT US

TIM CUSACK

Me Too

Copyright © 2012 by Tim Cusack

TC Publishing

First Edition 2012

The author is grateful for permission to use the following copyrighted material:

Cover design by Bambang Superman through 99designs.com
Cover photo by Fotolia, Steve Young, photographer, photo number 31342646
Interior design and typset by Katherine Lloyd, The DESK
Bio photo by Annie R Photography
printed at Color House Graphics, Grand Rapids, MI www.colorhousegraphics.com

Library of Congress Cataloging in Publication Data
Cusack, Timothy Michael
    Me Too: Extraordinary Everyday Stories that Connect Us / Tim Cusack
    ISBN: 978-0-9882506-0-4
Library of Congress control number: 2012949352

PRINTED IN THE UNITED STATES OF AMERICA

Printed on acid-free paper

To those who sense pain in others,
may you be a healing presence.

CONTENTS

EDITOR'S NOTE

I n a way, I think that the story of how Tim Cusack and I came to collaborate on this book is just like one of the stories that you will find herein; it's meaningful, serendipitous, and of course true...but I'll leave that story for Tim to tell.

After many years of being asked by audience members if he had a book that they could take home after a talk, Tim overcame his fear of writing and began scribing anecdotes from his life the old fashioned way, with a pen and yellow lined paper.

When we first met around the kitchen table in Tim's home, we couldn't have predicted where this would lead. It was something that neither of us had done before, but I can only say that we hit it off right away. We read through one of the stories, sat thinking for a minute, and then jumped into a discussion of what this piece would mean to people, what they could take away from it, and how they could apply it to their own lives.

I told Tim when we started this process, and I'll say it again here, that he did the hardest part: he took the first step. As a writer myself, I know that the most difficult part of a project is getting started, pushing aside your insecurities and the voice in your head that says, "You can't do this."

After a few months of sitting around that same table, two laptops in front of us, poring over documents and discussing life, death, and comma usage, I can say that these stories are presented to you exactly as Tim Cusack wants them to be. It's not your typical literary work. The writing is simple, straightforward, and in the style that Tim would tell them were you sitting around the house with him, drinking tea and talking about life.

Although each story is unique, there is a common theme that runs throughout the book. Whether light-hearted or serious, they are intended to provide lessons for life, and encourage the reader to draw on these lessons and reflect on their significance in his or her own life. They are not written in chronological order. This is not a biography, and therefore each chapter can be read on its own.

After getting to know Tim quite well, I can say with confidence that he has enough incredible stories to fill twenty books, but these are the ones that made the cut. Although he is a speaker by trade, many of these are experiences that he has never shared with audiences, but they are the moments in his life that came to him as he put pen to paper, and he bravely chose not to second-guess this process, and to share them with you.

Marie Lockerd—September 2012

Dirt Boy

His grandmother yelled yet again, "The school bus is waiting! If you don't hurry, it will leave without you!" Roy came running through the back door, through the family room, and into the kitchen. He grabbed his books off the counter, kissed his grandmother on the cheek, and said, "Love you, Gama." That's what he'd called her from the time he could talk.

The bus driver gave him a disgusted look and said, "Hey Roy, if I have to sit here for more than thirty seconds one more time, you're walking to school. I know your old grandma doesn't drive, so enjoy your walk, you little dirt boy."

Dirt boy. Roy heard that name at least 12 times a day now that he was in first grade. He spent six hours a day at school, and at least two kids per hour would tease him. Kids would say, "Don't sit next to me dirt boy," or "Don't touch my paper, dirt boy." It was true, Roy's hands were always dirty and so were his pants.

He would wipe his hands on his pants as he worked in his secret garden behind the wooden fence in the back yard of his grandmother's house.

Roy was just two years old when his parents died in a car accident. His grandmother was the only family member who wanted him. Roy's aunts and uncles thought he was a weird kid because he didn't talk. He didn't even seem to try. He wasn't interested in playing with toys or stuffed animals like most kids his age.

What he did seem to love was anything to do with a living plant—the grass in the lawn, a tree, a flower. He would sit next to a house plant and touch its leaves, trying to hold it, and at times causing it to spill over, getting dirt everywhere. Once when this happened, his uncle threw the plant out the back door next to a pile of firewood. Roy crawled out back and sat with the destroyed house plant. Even months later when his grandmother found him in that pile of wood, she noticed that the house plant was more alive, more colorful, than she'd ever remembered, and yet, its roots were exposed. She thought to herself, "How could this be?"

Roy's first grade teacher, Mrs. B, would have Roy wash his hands with soap and water before lunch, but his hands remained stained. "Roy," said Mrs. B, "Did you forget your lunchbox again?" Roy looked down at the floor, ashamed. There were many days he forgot his lunch. He would hide by the old oak tree, out of sight from the other kids, talking to the tree as if it were his best friend. He forgot his lunchbox because he was always running late, working in his secret garden. Mrs. B said, "Sit here at my desk. Here's an apple and some peanuts. I'll be back in a few minutes. You're staying in today, and I'm having a talk with your grandmother after school."

As Roy picked at his lunch, he was distracted by what he'd seen every day since coming into this classroom—a brownish, dying, potted tree in the back corner of the room. He didn't know what type of tree it was. It stood about three feet tall with medium sized leaves, maybe some kind of dwarf cherry or apple, he thought. Everyday he had wanted to tend to it, but didn't want to get caught playing in the dirt. Today he didn't care. He was alone. Roy stood up and walked toward the dying tree. As he got closer the tree's brown, shriveled leaves began to shake. He could see it moving as if a small breeze was blowing it.

With his small dirty hands, Roy touched the trunk of the tree at the point where it entered the soil. The color of the main trunk started turning from ash gray to a healthy dark brown. The leaves turned from their deathly shade into a deep emerald green. Small pink blooms began appearing out of buds that were never there before. The tree grew five feet taller than it was just seconds ago.

He heard the door open without warning. "Roy what are you doing?" asked Mrs. B. Roy couldn't lie. "It was dying. It just needed to be touched, to be held. It wanted to be loved." Mrs. B was in shock. She couldn't move. She couldn't believe what she was seeing. This old dying potted tree was more beautiful than any plant she had ever seen in her life.

Mrs. B said, "Roy, tell me the truth. Did you just touch that tree?" "Yes," said Roy. She walked over to him, sat down and said, "At home, at your grandmother's house, do you have plants?" "Yes," Roy said. "Is that why your hands are always so dirty?" Roy just looked at her. "After school today I'm going to drive you home. I want you to show me your plants."

Roy began to cry. He said, "I can't! It's a secret garden, and only me and my Mom and Dad know about it." With a soft, loving voice Mrs. B said, "What if you ask your Mom and Dad first to see if it would be alright if your grandmother and I could see your garden?"

Roy nodded his head in approval. That night after school, the gate on the fence that hid the garden opened. Roy saw Mrs. B and his grandmother standing in the back yard. He said, "It's okay for you to come in. My Mom and Dad said it's time to share what I've been growing."

Who Is Dirt Boy?

This story comes from an improv theater game called "build a story." You ask the audience for items to be incorporated into the story. In this case my audience consisted of my wife, Anne, who said "plant," and my daughter, Isabel, who gave me "lunchbox." With these two items in mind, I sat down for the next forty minutes and wrote this story.

After I finished writing "Dirt Boy," I thought about where it came from. Why did this spontaneous improvisational story unfold the way it did? Why did I make some of the choices that I did? One of the theories they teach in improv acting is that you have to be in the moment in order to use your intuition as a guide and produce those instances where everything just comes together in a way that you couldn't predict. If you get inside your head to try to figure out something clever, get a laugh, and make it about you, you'll miss the opportunity. When I wrote this story I was very much in the moment. It seemed to just flow out of me, almost outside of my control. It was like I was an observer of my mind's eye, watching it unfold before me. At times it was hard to move my pen fast enough to keep up with the words that were falling out on the page. At one point I cried as I wrote, surprised by where the story was going. With "Dirt Boy" I didn't intervene with it or attempt to edit it as I went along, I just tried to stay in the moment and let the story unfold.

It didn't take long for me to analyze this piece of art therapy. Under the surface I am Dirt Boy. I did get picked on in elementary school, but it was more about being short and vulnerable than about being dirty. I didn't have a secret garden, but I do remember taking long walks through my family's farm, with special areas that I thought of as mine, places I would go to think and be alone.

This seems to be pretty uniform among children. You can probably recall a room or outdoor fort or a special climbing tree that you felt was just yours. As a child, sitting in my secret places, I remember longing to be a healing presence, and to possess certain powers to help people who were hurting. In "Dirt Boy," Roy has a special ability to revive dying plants. Upon reflection I think that this was another form of me trying to work through the pain I experienced at school, and reflect on the special things about me that others didn't always see. Even as a child I identified with the archetype of the underdog, and sensed that I wanted to have a gift for helping others, especially those who needed it most.

As adults we still have secret gardens, private insights. We've all been a Dirt Boy at some time in our lives. It can be good to keep some things to ourselves and reflect on them. But at some point, it can also be healthy and beneficial to share the special moments in our lives with others, these pieces of our soul, just like Roy who eventually got up the courage to share his secret garden. I've been collecting stories, and the moments in them, for as long as I can remember. The garden of Dirt Boy is really about this collection of stories that I'm daring to scribe into a book. It's one thing to tell a few stories during my programs in front of a live audience, but to put them on paper for anyone to read and consume, without my verbal direction, is a much scarier and daunting concept for me. For years I was afraid that I wouldn't be able to transfer the significance of these stories from the spoken form to the written.

I believe they all have potentially healing powers and emotional insights, and I feel that sharing them is like sharing a very personal part of myself.

During a number of my speaking engagements, I've referenced my past as a hospice volunteer and the lessons I've taken away from being present with people at the end of life. I share the fact that in the end, most people just talk about a few moments, a few stories from their life. That's it...just a handful of experiences that are significantly meaningful.

That's what all these stories are to me: meaningful, inspiring, and true. My wish is that you will find these stories to be as refreshing, enriching, and life enhancing as they are for me. I hope that some of them will inspire you to step into your own secret soul garden and harvest some of those meaningful moments that can be shared with others.

I.
GOING FOR WHAT YOU WANT

You Know You Could Die, Right?

W hen facing the possibility of death which is completely out of your control, everything seems far away.

Gone was the protection of any feeling that my life, my fate, was in my hands. I was more than 5000 miles away from home and in a very dangerous place. At the time it felt like an impossible distance from home.

After struggling through my first year and a half of college, taking a job on a fishing boat in Alaska seemed like a reprieve. This was before *The Perfect Storm* or *The Deadliest Catch* brought the fierce lives of Alaskan fisherman into American living rooms, and yet I was warned of the danger I was heading into. This isn't the type of job that you fill out an application for. You have to know someone. My connection was an old family friend, Leon, the first mate on a crab boat that fished the freezing waters of the Bering Sea during the summer season. My "job interview" came in the form of a phone call from Leon. I was standing in the kitchen of the old farm house that I was renting, and at one point during our conversation I remember him asking me, "You know you could die, right?" He said that phrase. "You could die." At the time I was struggling with college, facing all my old academic failures, feeling like an outsider, a fake student. The "dying" word seemed almost like a good excuse at that time in my life.

I thought, "Well, that's one way to get out of going to college...

A professor would say, "Why isn't Tim showing up to class?"

"Oh, he died at sea."

"Oh, well, okay," the professor would say. "Let's carry on with class."

I hadn't seen Leon since I was in middle school. I remember him being a nice guy, a little pompous, a little bit of an ego, but for the most part he was pretty cool. His parents and my parents were good friends, so I figured he wouldn't deliberately put me in harm's way.

Despite Leon's warning about the perils of the job and short description of what it would entail, I didn't have a clue about what I was saying yes to. I think I visualized floating around on a boat, lowering down crab traps or "pots," pulling them up overflowing with the day's catch, and then going home to celebrate. I pictured myself watching beautiful sunsets and being sprayed with the ocean mist as it flew off the bow of the boat.

Needless to say, my expectations were naïve at best and totally out of touch with the reality of what happens on a fishing boat. After saying "yes"to my potential death sentence, I found myself in a foreign land. A Michigan farm boy like me stuck out like a sore thumb among Seattle based fisherman. The men I would be living and working with the next few months had been doing this for most of their adult lives. Hardened by life at sea, they were very rough, hard-edged, and they didn't seem too keen on making friends with the "Greenhorn," which they liked to call me. Initially they spent a lot of time teasing me about my complete inexperience in the job. One of their favorite "jokes" was to ask me, "Hey new guy, you're a farm boy, so you know what a *plow* is, right? It comes to a point in front? Well that's like a *bow*. It has a point."

Right guys, got it. Thanks for the tutorial.

During this time I heard the most "colorful" language I'd ever been surrounded by. My first greeting when I walked onto the boat was "Who the f*#% are you?" I came back with, "I'm Santa Claus, and if you keep saying naughty words I'm not going to bring you any presents this year." Two of the guys laughed, which was the only thing that saved me from being murdered by the "Mr. Naughty Word" man.

One of the things that initially surprised me the most was that everybody brought a gun with them. I couldn't imagine what they could possibly want to shoot out in the ocean. What I found out was that these guns were used alternately for poaching the sea wildlife and shooting holes in the bags of trash that were tossed into the ocean, which they referred to as, "the landfill."

There was an "every man for himself" type of atmosphere on the boat, and I didn't really feel safe around the guys. I had the general feeling that I always had to watch my back. Leon informed me later that at a certain point my coworkers had in fact started planning to get rid of me until he intervened.

To make matters worse, we were living in incredibly close quarters. When you didn't get along with someone it wasn't as if you could find some privacy. You had to deal with people whether you liked them or not.

There were times, when the catch was good or the weather was fair, that everyone would be in a good mood, which was especially true if the captain was happy. Of course the opposite was true too. If the captain wasn't happy you knew to stay out of the way.

Our captain did seem trustworthy, though. He was good at what he did. I also found some comfort in the strength of the boat that we would call home for the next several months. The vessel that we fished from was a 154 foot long steel monster, powering its way through thick ocean swells with two 16 cylinder Detroit diesel engines. The glass in the wheelhouse was three inches thick, thick enough to stop a bullet or, in our case, the giant waves that crashed over the bow of the boat during a storm. This metal beast seemed indestructible to me when I first stood on its deck, safely secured to the dock near shore. But when I found myself clasping the railing, faced with a 40 foot wall of dark grey water during a storm in the Bering Sea, it suddenly felt more like I was grasping onto a piece of cork set adrift in the ocean.

During one particularly bad storm I remember looking at those big Detroit motors that kept our boat moving and thinking, "I would give anything to be in a factory in Detroit right now, anything to be on solid ground again.'

We had a saying, "Red sky at night, sailor's delight. Red sky in the morning, sailors take warning." Depending on the color of the sky and the time of day, we could basically predict what kind of conditions would lie ahead. A storm during the day at sea is scary because you can see the water coming at you. You can even glimpse the next swell coming behind it, waiting its turn to pummel you. But at night in the darkness, a storm is ten times more terrifying. The lights of the boat only reach yards in front of you; just enough to know that in seconds you'll hit the next swell.

There was always a lingering thought in my head that if someone went overboard during the day you could find them, but at night they would just be lost. It's difficult to turn around in the ocean to pick someone up. You have to face the bow into the swell so the boat won't roll over, thus it's incredibly dangerous to make a turn. Facing a swell, the bow cuts into the bottom half of the swell and the rest crashes over it, causing the entire boat to shudder. It's like hitting a cymbal; the water hits the bow and then vibrates, resonating outward over the steel of the boat. It's similar to the sudden sense of losing control when you hit turbulence while flying. You know there are two pilots flying the plane, but if the turbulence is really bad, for a short period of time while you're being bounced around, it feels as if nobody is really in control... you're at the whim of the air current. In this case I was at the whim of the ocean, and as much as I respected my captain, I felt like we were helpless against the elements.

The vastness of the ocean is both beautiful and frightening in its immensity. You can't see the bottom. You can't see land. When you're out there, and you're rolling up and down over these swells, it seems beyond any power that you have ever known. That power of the ocean can't be contained. It's beyond comprehension.

The ocean dictates your fate. It doesn't care what happens to you. Unlike when we're threatened by conflicts in our day to day lives at home, you can't reckon or negotiate with the ocean. You can make excuses or negotiate with a professor in college, but not with the open sea.

There were times when the exhausting labor and the sleep deprivation drained me of any thought. There were also long stretches of hours when there was nothing to do, and it was in these times that I would contemplate what I was doing out here in the ocean. I remember visualizing how dying in the sea would go. I would flail around for awhile, treading water until I could continue no more. I would reach a point of fatigue, start to go under, lose my ability to breathe, close my eyes, and let myself die, eventually sinking to the bottom of the sea.

It was a lonely idea to be lost at sea. My existence suddenly felt insignificant in the face of such a nameless death, without even the comfort of a burial, a grave, something to be visited, cried over, flowers placed at. It seemed like such a waste to die like this. I spent a lot of time pondering the thought that I was going to die so far from home. My body would not be found. I would die at sea like so many people before me during wars, fishing trips, cruises, and rip tides.

During these long hours of down time or in the middle of a storm, I realized how important my life was to me, even though just months before I had flippantly thought that it would be a relief to die at sea...no big deal. I started to ask myself, "Why did I put myself in this place? Why did I think that it wouldn't happen to me?"

When you're in the middle of the ocean, there's not even a remote possibility of asking the captain, "Hey, you know what? This whole being on a boat thing, working long hours, bouncing around in the middle of nowhere is just not what I had in mind. I'd like to be dropped off on land now, please. Oh, and can you send my paycheck back to Michigan?"

At one point I fantasized about a scheme to fake appendicitis in order to get off the boat. I pictured myself being air lifted off the bow by a coast guard helicopter and being transported to a hospital. I figured I could fake my symptoms until I had a chance to slip out of my room and escape onto the streets of Seattle, my hospital gown flapping in the wind as I ran through the streets. The only problem with this plan was that I wouldn't be able to go straight home, because I couldn't stand the embarrassment of admitting that I couldn't handle the job I signed up for; I was just too weak. So I figured that until December rolled around I would get myself to Orlando, Florida and get a job at Disney World. I'd be dressed up as Mickey Mouse or maybe even Minnie Mouse, no one would recognize me and when the summer was done I could return home acting as though I'd been in Alaska the whole time, completely unfazed by the dangerous job. Of course I never followed through with this crazy plan, but the thoughts would come to mind when I was being washed with waves and feeling especially desperate and scared. All I could think was, "I want to be anywhere but here."

By looking for options in life, by experimenting with a variety of occupations it seems there's no way of avoiding the pain of experiencing what you don't want to do. It's like trying a dish of new food in order to understand that you don't like it. Someone can come close to describing it for you, but ultimately you have to try it for yourself.

The only possessions I brought from home were the clothes on my back. I had nothing else familiar that connected me to my life at home. I had nothing and no one to rely on. When facing possible death and having the time to processes it, I found myself looking inside for salvation.

I did make deals with God, too many to recall. My deals with God sounded like the same cliché lines that you see in the movies, "God, if you let me live, I promise I'll never do such and such again."Or, "God, if you let me live, I'll never lie or hurt anyone again. I'll be a better person: work with orphans in Africa (I subsequently did), save the planet (I recycle), and save the whales (I went to Sea World). Whatever you want, I'll do it."

Now, looking back at all this bargaining, it seems so crazy. God is in heaven, sitting in his big, gold-laden chair, listening to these pathetic deals I'm laying out. And, he's really thinking it over, scratching his big, full beard, nodding his head slightly and thinking to himself, "Okay, this is sounding pretty good. All I have to do is keep this boat upright? That's easy."

Even beyond making deals with God, the experience of coming so close to dying changes something inside your soul. That real sense of mortality, a little glimpse of the end of your life, changes everything from that day forward. I'm not sure what, or how it does. It's hard to describe the change. It's like the tectonic plates under the earth's crust, shifting ever so slightly. On the Richter Scale it could be a 1, yet it's changing, moving, altering everything. Once it moves, it never goes back to being the same ever again.

One night I lay in my bunk, trying to sleep through the gale outside, the waves throwing the boat around, not exactly being rocked to sleep when suddenly we hit a huge swell. I was tossed out of my top bunk onto the floor. The boat immediately hit another swell, causing me to slide across the sloped floor, hitting my head hard on the base of the wall. The impact made the sound of a cracking melon. I put my hand up to the spot where the pain was radiating from, and when I pulled it away I saw that it was covered in blood. Immediately the thought popped into my throbbing head, "Why don't you go back to school and learn how to read? Stop living a lie. You're gonna die you idiot!"

Obviously I've lived to tell the tale, and after the job was over that's exactly what I did; I went back to school and applied myself in a way that I never had before. In the end, despite the terror and hardship this voyage caused, I wouldn't take back the experience for anything. It reminded me of how precious life is and put my problems into perspective. It was the wake-up call that I needed.

What was I so worried about? I was having trouble in school? I didn't feel confident in my abilities? I hadn't found what I was good at yet? I didn't know what I wanted to do for a career? After being whipped around in a floating death trap all summer I realized that those things aren't the end of the world. Dying on a fishing boat *is* the end of the world...literally the end of my world.

After my experience on the fishing boat, I tackled my problems with the knowledge that no matter what happened, even if I struggled and failed, I had my life. I could take control of it, and every night I could watch the sunset with both feet planted firmly on the ground.

Bingo! I Changed the World

Have you ever wished, prayed, or hoped for something to happen so strongly that your entire being was wrapped up in that one moment? You felt like you needed to change the immediate circumstance you found yourself in, and the only way to make this happen was through sheer will power. You didn't say a word, you kept it to yourself. It was up to you to change everything.

At the time, I was a young boy growing up on a farm. Our church was hosting a bingo night. Guess what religion? This wasn't just any bingo night. In this old Irish Catholic community it was called Potluck Bingo Night. Everyone participating had to bring something to be given away. It could be anything from cupcakes to a shovel. Instead of cash prizes for winning at Bingo, you would earn items that people had donated from their farms, homes, or something that was lying around in the backyard.

As we prepared for that night, my dad started looking around for things of value that we could offer to the potluck. He settled on a basket of farm grown produce, a loaf of bread baked fresh that day by my mother, and lastly, one of our prized roosters. This wasn't all just charity. The potluck offered an opportunity for the men to show off their best livestock, and the women to exhibit their culinary abilities.

The rooster that my father chose to offer at this event wasn't just any rooster...it was *my* rooster. My rooster was one of the biggest, strangest, most beautiful, multicolored roosters you've ever seen. When he turned his neck he almost looked like a pheasant. However, he was a vicious creature, part fighting chicken, part tiger, and also the Don Juan of the chicken coop. Once, my brother Danny was attacked for stepping too close to the hen house by this rooster's especially large talons. When I say *my* rooster, what I mean is that on the farm we children would sort of claim certain animals. We would say, "That's my cow, or my cat," so although these weren't traditional pets that you could actually hold in your lap and sleep with at night, to me this was 'my rooster.' His name was Big Boy.

It can get tricky when you start naming farm animals, because you can be petting your steer one day and eating him the next. When you claim a living thing as yours by giving it a name, it cements an emotional attachment. That attachment happens so quickly, so easily, so effortlessly. The feeling wasn't there just seconds ago. Now suddenly you have this thing—a puppy, a ring, a toy—that you've become entirely attached to within seconds. I loved this rooster from the moment I saw him and immediately claimed him as mine.

I begged my dad to choose a different chicken for Pot Luck Bingo. I couldn't believe that he would give away my rooster, which in my eyes was no longer a farm animal but a pet. Because he looked so amazing, he was truly a creature of value, or he would make a great chicken dinner, my Dad wouldn't budge from choosing Big Boy to be a prize at Potluck Bingo Night. Whatever his fate, I knew that no one would love him like I did. I remember my dad put him in a big burlap bag along with the other goods, and we headed out.

All I could think about was losing my rooster to someone who didn't know him. Someone who didn't love him like I did. We would be separated forever.

At the church hall I sat looking down at my bingo card as the letters and numbers were being called out. My rooster was proudly displayed in the front of the room for all to see. He was the last item of the night, sort of the grand prize. Our cards were filling up fast. I only needed one more number. I was filled with nervous anticipation, dreading that at any moment someone would yell out "BINGO!" and take my chicken away from me.

I tried to muster up all the powers of the universe to will the winning number into being. "G24. G24. G24. Please God, let it be G24. Give my rooster back to me where he belongs."

The basket was rolled. A number was pulled...

On the way home that night, sitting in the dark of the back seat of our family van next to my rooster, I cried tears of triumph. Through the power of my will and a little help from God, I had changed the world.

Empty Halls

The assembly was a smashing success. In comedy terms, "I killed" in front of 250 K-5th grade students. We had lots of laughs as well as some very serious moments about human truths that even elementary kids understand and love to be reminded of...truths like: we all have feelings, sometimes we feel sad, hurt, scared, and excited. When I share these types of truths, elementary children consistently sit on the gym floor absolutely still. I can tell that they are all thinking to themselves: "Me too. Me too. I'm normal. I get it. Oh, good. That's a relief. Okay, move on! Tell another funny story. Make me laugh. I need an emotional break, speaker guy!" Now, after the assembly is over, I'm sitting alone on a chair just outside the school office. The halls are empty and quiet.

There's something special about a vacant school hallway. Even as a young kid I loved the feeling of an empty school. I hated school as a student. I was a horrible academic. Recess offered a temporary distraction from the inevitable reality of sitting while the teacher talked, my mind wandering, fantasizing about some great future achievement that existed only in my head. But there was something about the smell, the lack of noise, the institutional stillness of an empty school that I just loved. I remember being in an empty school building during the summer when no one was around. I knew I could be there with no responsibility and that felt so good. There would be no one nagging me about undone homework or papers not written or books left unread.

Just seeing an empty classroom is pleasant to me...little desks, books stacked on tables, smeared chalk on the blackboard, the globe that sits untouched. I can never remember a time during all my school days that my friends and I, or other kids, sat and pondered the globe. Being raised in a small rural town in the Midwest, the idea of going to another country seemed out of reach. The globe might as well have been another planet, and in our classroom it sat relatively undisturbed. My friends and I never asked each other, "Where would you go if you could?" If I had been asked my answer would have been, "Anywhere but this classroom." Instead of examining geography we competed at how fast we could spin the globe on its metal axis, pretending we could make everyone in the world so dizzy they would puke.

That day, as I sat enjoying the quiet of the empty halls, out of thin air a young boy appeared in front of me, a little guy, maybe 2nd or 3rd grade, standing just inches from my face. In his left hand he held a balled-up piece of yellow legal paper and in his right hand a broken, chewed-up, yellow, number 2 pencil.

He stuck both hands out at me and said, "Sign my autograph!"

It took a few seconds, but I said, "What?"

He said again with the same flat-out order, "Sign my autograph!"

I'm thinking to myself, "Sign this boy's autograph? Oh! What he's really saying is he wants *my* autograph."

Just to be sure I said, "Do you want me to sign my name for you?"

"Yes, sign my autograph!" He said this in a tone of, "What

don't you understand about signing an autograph? Man, are you stupid or something?"

The almighty autograph! I've never really figured out the autograph thing. What is it about having someone we admire sign their name to a piece of paper, a book, a photo, or our forehead? I suppose we somehow feel that we have a little piece of that person that is ours to keep, or a personal connection, that famous person wrote something special just for me. That's what the little guy wanted from me! My name written on a piece of paper. Most of the time I've told students they didn't need my autograph, that I should be getting theirs. This usually brings a weird look.

But for some reason I didn't do that this time. I took the crushed ball of paper and unfolded it to the point where I could write my name, took his hepatitis C covered pencil and asked, "What's your name?"

"Tony," he replied.

I wrote, "To Tony, from Tim." Then I wrote, "Be good." I wasn't sure why I added that, but I did. I handed the paper and pencil back to him.

He looked at it, smiled, then looked me in the eye and said, "Did you really get in trouble when you were in school?"

"Yes," I said. He nodded his head in an understanding way.

He started to walk off, then stopped, looked back at me straight in the eye and asked, "Did you really have a hard time reading?"

"Yes."

"Me too," he said.

He smiled at me, then turned and ran down the hall, I was hoping, back to a classroom. As I watched Tony turn the corner at the end of the hall, I heard the principal come up behind me. "What did he want?" the principal asked.

"That was Tony. He wanted my autograph."

The principal responded with a disgusted look and said, "He's the worst kid in this school."

I was stunned! I responded by saying, "Really? I've got a couple more labels for you. I think he's probably one of the more emotional kids in this school, and a risk taker." The principal and most likely many teachers had labeled him the "worst," but out of all the kids in this school, this little guy was so moved, that he either got permission to leave class, or didn't, but he took action. He found me and asked two very personal questions. He needed confirmation. He needed to know that he had gotten it right. He wanted an affirmation that his soul counted. He needed to reconnect personally and privately.

~

As adults I think we lose the willingness and the guts to do what Tony did. There are times when we're moved emotionally and spiritually, but we're too afraid to take the action, to get up from our desk, to leave the house and get the affirmation our soul needs to hear...to know what we're feeling is right. It's scary to trust that urge, to take that risk.

Trusting intuition and instincts can be a risky act. One of the most common excuses for not taking the time to attend to our soul is that we're too busy. We have more important things going on. Really? What's more important than our soul? Oh yeah, our car, house, job, social status. But if we don't tend to our soul, what do we have to offer to our families, coworkers, and personal projects that we claim to be so busy with?

In a very humble way, even if it's with a crumpled piece of paper and a broken crayon, get up and get the autograph you need. Ask the questions you have. It doesn't matter what the principal (or the world) thinks, if it's what you need to do.

Tony, when I signed your autograph, I told you to "Be good." I'm sorry. What I meant to say was, "Be yourself."...but you already knew how to do that.

Beginner's Mind: Act I

BE MY DAD

This play recounts events as they truly occurred.

(Tim Cusack just finished performing an assembly at an elementary school where he told a variety of children's stories. He moved from the auditorium to the second grade classroom to do a follow-up workshop. Tim stands in front of a classroom of twenty five students).

TIM

What did you see me do that you'd like to learn how to do to help you with your acting and story telling?

(Half a dozen hands eagerly shoot up in the air).

LITTLE GIRL

How did you talk like a bear?

TIM

First you have to become a bear. You have to ask yourself, "How does a bear walk? How would a bear move? How would a bear scratch his back?" Then, after you've moved around for a while as a bear, and you know what it feels like, how would your bear talk?

(Tim speaks in the bear's voice again. All the kids laugh. Tim picks the next hand).

LITTLE BOY

How do you make things look like they're there when they're not?

TIM

Well, you don't *pretend* to open a door. You really see the door knob and really grab the handle as if it's a real door, but it's not really there. You're just using the space around you to create any object you want. So, no matter what the object is, you just have to think, "How would your hands hold that object or that thing you want to use," and if you really see it, so will the audience.

(Tim picks the next hand).

LITTLE BOY #2

Would you be my dad?

TIM

Excuse me? What did you say?

LITTLE BOY #2

Would you be my dad?

(Tim is taken aback and pauses for what seems like a light year, scanning his mind for a response. He's tempted to ask, "Well, what's your Mom look like?" but he refrains).

TIM

Well, I can't do that.

LITTLE BOY #2

Why not?

TIM

Because I'm married.

LITTLE BOY #2

Get divorced.

TIM

I can't do that.

(Again, on the inside, Tim is scrambling for the best way to get out of the situation without hurting Little Boy #2's feelings or traumatizing the classroom).

TIM

You know, you seem like a really good guy, and I would love to be your dad. As a matter of fact, I think I would be proud to be your dad. But, I can't because I don't live here. I live pretty far from here, so it just wouldn't work. I'd be lucky to be your dad if I could. (Little Boy #2 smiles and looks around the room at his classmates with a look of pride and satisfaction).

TIM

Next question. *Again*, what did you see me do that you want to learn how to do?

Thoughts on "Be My Dad"

I think it's safe to say that many young boys see their fathers as the ultimate embodiment of masculinity. They enjoy watching their dad shave his face in the morning. They want to follow him around while he repairs something and examine his tools. Little children like to argue with their friends about whose dad is stronger, faster, smarter, and cooler.

I don't want to assume that the little boy who asked me to be his dad didn't have a father in his life, but it seems to me that he was probably missing something. He probably saw me as someone who would be a fun dad and a good dad. He could see himself spending time with me and just being around me.

The beginner's mind can fantasize about how great something could be. Without second guessing itself, it leaps over any practical barriers that would prevent it from getting what it wants. The beginner's mind doesn't dwell on what it can't do. It didn't even occur to the little boy to think of his question as being inappropriate. It was just a very honest question, even though it was extremely personal.

For the beginner's mind it's a simple yes or no question. Will you be my dad?

Just get divorced and we'll live happily ever after as father and son.

A beginner's mind doesn't edit love much. The beginner's mind feels love deeply and quickly and often doesn't waste time thinking about it in an abstract way. It's very concrete. One who thinks with a beginner's mind can quickly fall in love with a bug or a shell or a rock and instantly there's an attachment. They don't want to let it go. "Put that rock down. Leave it here." "No! I love it. I want it to be mine."

When the beginner's mind loves something, it simply asks for it. No reservations, no shame.

Thank you, Little Boy #2.

THE END

II.

BEING THERE

A Critical Ride

When cycling with a group, you take turns in the slipstream of the rider just ahead of you. They're breaking the solid, still air in front of you, creating a vacuum that takes about 30% less effort to maintain the same speed. On a 50 mile bike ride, this percentage of reduced effort makes a huge difference. However, because you're riding just inches behind another cyclist, this benefit also creates some risk. If you're riding at 20+ mph, the slightest mistake—braking or a sudden flat tire—can cause severe repercussions. The benefits of the slipstream can also create an opportunity for disaster.

I had just glanced at my speed. Our pack of 40 riders was pedaling about 21 mph, just getting warmed up for a long ride. We were all riding two abreast on the side of a paved, flat country road. It was an incredibly hot and humid evening in the middle of July.

As our pace picked up, I thought to myself, "This is going to be one of those fast, hard, hammer rides." That's when I heard a loud bang, followed by another bang that was even louder. These two sounds did not make sense in my brain. It was the noise associated with a car crashing, but something was missing. Then I heard the missing piece. Tires screeching on dry pavement. All this sound was coming from just yards behind me. The pack of riders suddenly slowed to turn around and see what had happened.

A rider was lying face down in the middle of the road. There was no bike in sight. A gray pick-up truck was lying at an angle in a ditch just beyond.

To this day, I'm not sure what really happened. I heard that someone flatted. I heard that someone clipped the back wheel of the rider ahead of them. I heard that someone lost control. Whatever the reason, there was a crash in the pack of riders that started an inevitable chain reaction The riders behind the crash veered out of the way as bikes slowed in front of them. The rider who was hit must have seen this chaos unfolding and instinctively swerved out of the way of the domino effect of careening bikes in front of him. It's only natural to avoid a crash happening in front of you, but he turned too sharply to the left and ended up in the lane of oncoming traffic. It was estimated that the pick-up that hit him was traveling at 50+ mph, striking him head on.

The first bang I had heard was the rider hitting the truck's grille. The second bang was the rider hitting the windshield—then screeching tires followed by silence. Once everyone came to a stop these horrible noises were still echoing in my ears, but on the outside for a few seconds, the whole world seemed deathly quiet.

Immediately, calls to 911 were made. The severity of the accident was immense. Our rider lay face down, bleeding, motionless except for the small rise and fall of his chest. He was alive, but we all knew that the long term prognosis would be life-altering at best.

My first instinct was to help somehow. Other riders had stopped oncoming traffic. Some stood staring helplessly at our fallen friend. As I scanned the scene, I noticed that the pick-up had left black skid marks running into the ditch. One of our female riders was sitting next to a woman on the bank of the ditch, who I assumed to be the driver of the truck. My mind flooded with thoughts. What is the driver experiencing right now? Disbelief, shock, guilt, anger, confusion? Probably too many emotions to process.

In my study of psychology in college, we weren't taught how to handle anything like this. Post college I had attended crisis intervention and psychodrama trainings, but even with this work, it's hard to be prepared for moments like this. Ironically, four days from this accident, I would be attending a three day workshop on the topic of crisis management. As I started walking toward the driver of the truck, I couldn't help but think about how useful that workshop would have been to me in this situation.

Critical incident stress management training, known as CISM, offers guidelines for how to assist those involved in a crisis situation like a shooting, a tornado, a mass flooding, or any tragic event that is out of a person's control. The stress that results from these traumas needs to be addressed in some way, and in most cases the sooner the better.

There's a formula that's referred to as E+R=O which stands for Events + Response = Outcome. Most of the time we have no control over the events in our lives, but we do have control over how we respond to those events. The response will dictate the type of outcome we get.

At the time of the crash, what I did know from my past training was that one way to start the healing process was to allow the person to tell their story of what happened, or what they think happened. What I learned later at the crisis management workshop is that this can be considered the first step in the three step process known as CISM.

Step 1: Ventilate. This step is called "ventilate" because its aim is to let the person get it all out. To begin, you let the person give their view of the incident, what they saw, what they heard, anything that they can remember. By letting someone tell their story, they hear for themselves, out loud, what happened. At first all that matters are the facts. Often people will tell the story multiple times, each time recalling the incident with more detail.

Step 2: Validate. This step is meant to communicate to the person that you hear what they're saying, that what they're feeling is right. Here they move from talking about the facts of the situation to how they are feeling about it. One way to start is by asking yourself how you would feel if this event happened to you. How would you feel? Sad, scared, guilty, all of them at once? When it comes to the emotions of the person who has been through a trauma, it's not about wrong or right; whatever emotions they're experiencing, you validate that it makes sense for them to be feeling that way. It's important to remember that you can never predict what feelings will come. Every person responds differently to a crisis situation. One technique is to ask the very basic question, "How are you feeling right now? Tell me what happened." If they can, the person will tell you. Some emotions may be hidden or masked, but if you listen and trust your gut, you'll hear it. If you repeat back an emotion, and it's not really an accurate description of what they're feeling, they'll let you know. Just go with the feelings they give you.

Step 3: Educate. This means that when you've finished debriefing someone in a crisis, you identify what it is that they will walk away with...what they have learned about their feelings and perhaps what they can expect in the days and weeks to come. Depending on the level of the trauma and the individual person's reaction to it, you might inform them that they will probably keep replaying the event in their mind, maybe even lose sleep or experience a loss of appetite. Regardless, they need to walk away knowing that what they're feeling is named. This is when the word "normal" comes into play. No matter how someone is feeling after a trauma, you let them know that it's normal. It's normal to be upset and overwhelmed for awhile. The two most common emotional reactions associated with any type of critical incident are *anger* and *guilt*. These are incredibly normal and appropriate reactions.

Walking closer to the driver, I knew she was experiencing trauma. To say she needed "help" was an understatement. She needed an intervention: a companion, a listener, someone to talk to, an ally and a supporter; someone to be there for her at that moment. I knew that overwhelming emotions flooded her brain and body. She needed help to process her overloaded nervous system.

As I stepped down into the ditch next to this woman, I didn't know the CISM steps, but as I look back, my instinctual reaction to the situation basically followed this outline. At the time I mostly knew that she just needed someone to be with her, to be on her side, to know that she was not going to have to go through this trauma alone. Mostly I could act as a temporary companion and ally. When I initially sat down next to her she was in a state of shock, staring straight ahead, dumbfounded. As she gradually came out of her shock, she became intent on getting a hold of someone she knew to come and be with her. Her hands shook as she dialed number after number on her cell phone. Clearly she was desperate for some comfort and support.

I turned to her and asked what happened. At first she simply replied, "I don't know. I don't know what happened." Her memory of the incident was hazy, and initially the only thing she could recall was narrowly missing a road sign as she plowed into the ditch. She remembered nothing about the rider who had struck her truck. Then, slowly, her thoughts became more organized. She started describing the shock that she experienced when the rider "came out of nowhere." She spoke of how he suddenly appeared in front of her, and she had no time to swerve to avoid him.

Between the riders' observations of what had happened and the police forensics team, it became clear that there was no way she could have avoided this tragic incident. There was a woman rider at the scene who had witnessed everything. She voiced to me that there was nothing the driver could have done. I encouraged her to say that to the driver who started crying upon hearing it wasn't her fault, that there was nothing she could have done to avoid it.

I'm sure that the driver of this pick-up was experiencing a massive amount of guilt, even though there wasn't any way she could have avoided hitting the rider. Like a deer darting out of nowhere, it was truly an accident. The reality of it was that the driver just hit someone and may have killed them. Guilt is real. It's important to name that guilt.

The other emotional component, anger, comes from the question "Why?" Why did this happen to *me*? Why did this guy ride out in front of *my* car? The most common series of thoughts for those involved in a critical incident are "would've," "could've," "should've." If only I *could've* left a few seconds earlier or later, this incident would have never happened, and everything would have been different. I *should've* seen him coming and swerved out of the way sooner. It's good to remind people that it's normal to think this way, to wish that you could change the situation.

If you're ever involved in a critical incident like this, you might experience an incredibly common phenomenon referred to as survivor's guilt. All the other riders, including me, were left with a sense of guilt. This, too, is a normal emotional reaction to being part of a critical incident. It could have happened to any one of us, but it didn't. I survived. I got to go home. I got to see my wife, my kids, and my friends again. I got to live, and because of that, I felt guilty.

Another phenomenon that occurs in conjunction with a tragic situation like this one is what's called "The Ripple Effect." Similar to dropping a pebble in water, a wave of emotions ripples outward through the people who are involved in the unfortunate event. The people involved are affected, as are the witnesses, who then tell their friends and family about it, who in turn then tell someone else. When we riders returned home, we involved our families in the incident. Without knowing it, our loved ones had to naturally, and in their own way, provide some version of the CISM process with us. We needed to tell our story of what had happened, and we needed someone to listen.

Our fellow rider died a few days later. About a month after the accident I got a call from the driver of the pick-up. She was so grateful for the time I spent with her, so thankful to me for being there.

These critical incidents won't always be as extreme as a tragic death. We can employ the three steps of CISM in our daily lives with our loved ones, co-workers, or even strangers who seem to be having a bad day. You might not even reach step two, and that's okay. Simply letting the person "ventilate," describe their experience and express their feelings, might be all you have time for, and that alone is very helpful. When we see someone on the side of the road, who's just been in a fender bender, or when our spouse comes home upset over a conflict at work, or our child has a fight with a friend, we can be of real assistance to them by acting as a sounding board. Just ask what happened and how they are feeling; express your sympathy; say "I'm so sorry." Let them know that it's okay to feel whatever it is that they're feeling. Even the mildest of situations can leave a person feeling guilt and anger, and that's to be expected.

If you ever find yourself involved in a critical incident, and you can't recall the three steps, just be there. Remember, this is not therapy. You don't need a Master's degree or Ph. D. to listen to someone. You don't have to physically hold someone to comfort them. You don't need to fix the situation. You just need to be present. A phrase to remember in these times is, "Listen more, talk less." Allowing someone to express their emotions is the start of healing.

Planting a Seed

Most of you have probably heard of the psychological term, "repressed memory." It's usually caused by some type of trauma, which results in the suppression of the memory of a bad experience and the emotional pain that came with it. In my case, many little emotional traumas occurred in relation to school, and caused me to repress memories from my early life. There are some experiences, however, that stuck with me despite their painful nature.

My earliest memory of school is my first day of kindergarten. I can only recall a few experiences after that, all the way through high school. When my mom tried to drop me off on that first day I held onto her like a little monkey hanging from a tree. There were too many kids, too much noise, and all of it seemed like pure chaos to my young mind.

Think about the walls of a kindergarten classroom; the alphabet, numbers, posters, cut-outs of different shapes in different colors. For me it was just too much stimulation. I was completely overwhelmed. My brain couldn't process all this novelty. I remember thinking, "Take me home. Get me out of this place that makes me feel so anxious and out of control." My brain already started shutting down on that first day.

I do remember one good thing from that time. After overhearing the other kids teasing me about being short, my kindergarten teacher put her arm around me and said with a smile, "Good things come in small packages." She let me go, and I ran to the bathroom to be alone and try to figure out what she meant by this. I knew it was something profound, so I kept repeating it to myself... "Good things come in small packages." Then it hit me: a diamond ring! It's one of the most prized gifts in the world, and it comes in a small package. I'm like a diamond ring! I thought to myself, "Yeah, take that you creeps. I'm extremely valuable, so back off!"

After that I must have begun to repress the traumatic experiences that I had throughout my school years, as well as the normal, everyday experiences that went along with them, because that's almost all I remember until maybe 7th grade. I guess my brain was trying to protect me from recalling all the major traumas that I experienced in relation to my education. The few things I do remember are mostly bad. I remember standing in front of the class trying to do a math problem on the blackboard, everyone rolling their eyes, laughing, mocking me. I recall trying to read out loud, being ridiculed, having my spelling test results read out loud (9 out of 10 words wrong!) Once a teacher hit me over the head with a textbook. Mainly I remember sitting at my desk, feeling lost, confused, and just not getting it, hour after hour, day after day, and year after year.

My performance was so poor that I was pulled out of class to go to a special room with a speech teacher. Although I knew this meant that I wasn't doing as well as the other kids, it was a ray of light in my day. Even this positive memory is hazy; the only thing

I recall is that the teacher had some toys to play with, and she was kind of pretty and really nice to me.

I remember thinking, "Why can't school be like this? Just me and one teacher. No one picking on me. Just quiet, thoughtful moments, feeling like I was normal, that I could do things right because she said so every time I saw her." That feeling of accomplishment wouldn't last long though; all I had to do was walk back into my regular classroom for it to be ripped away from me.

I hit bottom in my sophomore year of high school. First of all, in my private defense for such bad grades—I was in love! Her name was Sheila Roberts. She was one of, if not the most beautiful girl in the entire high school. I wasn't the only guy who thought that, even senior guys would agree with me.

My report card came back with five "F's" and one "C." The C was probably in gym class. My parents sat me down and asked if I was doing drugs. "No," I said. I was secretly doing a little alcohol on the weekends to kill the pain, but I didn't really enjoy getting high, just drunk. It helped me forget about school...being overwhelmed, lost, not getting it, not understanding. To make matters worse, I kept all of this a secret. Day after day I attended school and acted like nothing was wrong—joking, laughing with friends, getting in trouble in class, being sent to the office, all the while pretending that I didn't care about any of it. The office was better than the classroom. Mrs. Pennington, the office secretary, had a jar of candy for kids she felt sorry for. Let's just say I got a lot of candy.

On the inside, where people couldn't see, I carried the weight of a huge secret; I couldn't write, spell, read, or do math. I was a walking lie! A fraud! I came to school every day, but couldn't really do my job as a student.

Carl Jung theorized that humans function best when what

they feel on the inside matches what they appear to be on the outside. He called this "congruency." If only I could have read this, (literally, if only I actually knew how to read), or had someone tell me about this concept. Better yet, how wonderful would it have been if a teacher, a counselor, *someone*, had identified my behavior as being the result of psychological and emotional trauma, and let me know that all of these overwhelming emotions were normal, that they were just a sign that I needed to ask for help. I could have been spared a lot of pain. But, that didn't happen.

The closest I ever came to realizing what it's like to have an adult help me and show me that they believed in me was in my junior year when we had a new band teacher, Mr. Bennett. He was a suit-wearing, well groomed, serious guy who started our first day off by announcing that everyone starts with an "A." "Holy crap," I thought. "Who is this guy? Apparently he hasn't read my rap sheet, because I'm not an 'A' kinda guy." He said, "I work on the pip demerit system. One pip equals a quarter of a grade. Four pips will lower your grade one whole level." When he said this, I looked at the clock and wondered to myself, "How many pips could I get in one hour? I bet I could get that "A" down to a "C" by the end of this class. I think I acquired a few pips that first day, but Mr. Bennett knew that there was something behind my bad behavior.

We practiced our marching on the street in front of school. It was a form of marching called Drum and Bugle Corp, which was all new to us. It wasn't really my kind of thing. The structure turned me off...standing at attention, heels together, feet pointed out at forty-five degree angles, quickly turning left face, right face, about face. Mr Bennett would bark out directions like a drill sergeant—way too military for me.

I started dancing around, mocking the way we were marching.

Mr. Bennett didn't find it amusing. He stopped everything, came over to me, and yelled "Left Face!" I did it, but not the way he wanted. Again, "Left Face!" He drilled me until I caved.

I was so angry with him. I wasn't going to be singled out like this. After class, I put my coronet in the instrument closet and walked into his office, ready to yell at him. Before I could start he said,

"Oh, Tim, I'm glad you're here. I want to talk to you. Close the door and have a seat." He continued, "I'm looking for a new drum major."

Is this guy nuts? I came in here to tell him off, and now he's consulting with me about finding a new drum major. What the heck is going on?

He said, "I think I found one."

"Really? Who do you have in mind?"

"You."

"Me? You want me to lead the band?" Then Mr. Bennett, the master teacher, the psychotherapist, said, "You're a smart ass, Tim. You're a ham, and you know it. We have five parades this year, as well as the University of Michigan band day. You want to show off? Well, is that enough people for you?" I was stunned. How did he get to know me so well in such a short amount of time? We never even talked, but yet he seemed to know more about me than I did. He saw me as a performer, saw my "acting out" as simply "acting," and he used my talent to benefit us both!

I led our band as drum major that year, and I took it very seriously. Suddenly, I was the one reprimanding people for screwing around. I adopted the attitude that teachers had always taken with me of "I can't believe the behavior of some of these kids." I would tell them to knock it off. This is my band. We've got to be good. No excuses.

When I came back for my senior year, Mr. Bennett was gone, replaced by Mr. VanDyke, who couldn't have been more different. I lasted about three weeks before the new teacher kicked me out. Just a year earlier I had led the band. Now I was back to my old ways, standing outside the open door to the band room during class, yelling with a German accent, *"VanDyke, vee know you're in zere. Come out vith your hans up!"* Then I'd run down the hall before he could catch me.

Fortunately, even though Mr. Bennett was gone, he had already made an impression on me. While he was still my teacher he told my mom something at Parent Teacher Conferences that I never forgot. That night after meeting with my teachers, my mom came home and yelled at me about how none of them liked me. She said, "You talk during class. You get into trouble. Your behavior is appalling."

Then, she said, "Oh, by the way, Mr. Bennett told me that he thought you would do great things someday." My stomach dropped. I drifted out of the kitchen into my bedroom, closed the door, put a pillow over my head, and began to cry. The guy who really knows me, who can see through my act, thinks I will do great things someday!? Oh my God, what if he's right? No one had ever said anything like this about me before. I was sixteen years old, old enough to understand what it meant to have someone see something in me that could be great. This man that I admired so much thought that *I*, me, Tim Cusack, bad student, could matter to this world...I could make a difference. Mr. Bennett wouldn't say it if he didn't mean it. He said it, so it must be true.

Isn't it amazing, absolutely astounding, how one person's words can mean so much? Words of praise and encouragement stay with you, especially when they come from the right person at the right time. His belief in me inspired me to live up to his expectations. He planted a seed in my soul that grew over the years. His statement became part of who I am and pushed me to try to accomplish the great things that he said I would.

Twenty years later I was giving a talk at a school in Michigan's upper peninsula, and I got to talking to a band teacher after the show. I ended up telling him about my experience with Mr. Bennett and how much his support and encouragement meant to me. The teacher urged me to contact Mr. Bennett, knowing that, as an educator, it's nice to hear that you've made a difference in a student's life. He provided me with the Michigan directory of band teachers, and I decided to dial up my old teacher.

A guy answered the phone. "Hello?"

"Are you Mr. Bennet?"

"Yes."

"Are you a band teacher?"

"Yes."

"Do you remember a long time ago a student by the name of Tim Cusack."

Long pause. "*Oh yes....*"

In fact, he went on to tell me that he had thought of me just two weeks earlier. He was moving into a new house when an old yearbook fell out of a box he was carrying and opened to a page with my picture on it. The synchronicity of this occurrence after twenty years of no contact made me feel even better about having made the call. I continued by telling him, "You told my mom that I would do great things someday."

He jokingly responded with, "I did?"

I retorted, "You better have because I've held onto that for years. I believed you."

"I'm sure I did."

I thanked him for believing in me and making a difference in my life.

I don't remember much from Kindergarten through 12th Grade, but all I really needed to hear and remember was that I would do great things someday. His words were the beginning of a new way of looking at myself. Mr. Bennett did what no other educator was willing or able to do. He set aside the time to examine why I behaved the way I did. By doing this, he gained insight into me and helped me channel my skills into something positive. By believing in me and voicing his observation to my mother, he planted a seed in me that never stopped growing.

You're Not Alone

There are a few times in life when we need help the most. Two of the biggest ones are 1) when we're *coming* out, greeting the world as freshly born babies, and 2) when we're *going* out, taking our last breaths of life.

He was really thin, what they mean when they say "skin and bones," very old, very frail. He could no longer keep his eyes open. He looked completely helpless, lifeless...because he was.

My first task as a hospice volunteer was not even close to what I expected. I had envisioned sitting alongside someone, in a pleasant living room, having a lovely chat. Instead I found myself awkwardly feeding a dying old man who was lying in a hospital bed. The head of the bed was angled up so it would be easier to feed him, let gravity do its work. The nurse showed me how to take a spoon, scoop it into one of two little bowls of what looked to be baby food, one dark brown and one light brown, and touch the spoon to his bottom lip—that's his cue to open his mouth if he's ready to eat more.

The first time I touched his bottom lip and he opened his mouth I had a feeling of accomplishment. He took a small amount off the spoon, some of the food falling outside his mouth.

"Just like feeding a baby," I thought. I grew up in a large family, the third oldest of ten children. I remember feeding baby food to my younger siblings and wiping mouths many years ago. But this man was no baby, he just needed the same care as one.

I tried my best to get this right, to feed him, care for him, knowing that he didn't have a future, no more potential...it's the end of his life. It struck me as being the opposite of feeding and caring for a baby. Babies are helpless, yet so full of endless possibilities, becoming more human every second, making noises not quite words, looking right into your eyes. I remember feeding my own babies and wondering what they were thinking about. The way they would gaze back at me, I sometimes wondered, "Who's the most intelligent person in the room right now? Is it me, the feeder, or the little person wearing a bib with food all over his face with a look of, 'Hey buddy, someday you'll understand, you'll get it. Maybe, we'll see. Now hand me my sippy cup and back off.'"

The experience of feeding your own babies is disconcerting in the sense that you don't really know what you're doing at first, but at least with your children you have a feeling of comfort in knowing that they are yours, part of you. When I had my first experience in hospice, feeding this dying man, I had a painfully awkward feeling that I had never quite experienced. I had never been with a dying person before. In medical terms he was shutting down. He was literally in his last days. No nurse or fellow volunteer could have prepared me for this feeling or have gotten me through it. I had to be in it and experience it on my own.

Often in life when we find ourselves in uncomfortable or painful situations, our first instinct is, "How do I make this stop?" When you find yourself in these awkward situations, with intense discomfort, there's a sense of vulnerability in truly not knowing what you're doing and a fear of screwing up. An inner voice tells you that you're going to get it wrong, or god forbid, maybe even hurt someone because of your lack of ability or intelligence. When we don't know what to do in an uncomfortable situation it's hard to trust the process. In these types of experiences there is no instruction manual. In times like this we turn to our gut, our intuition, for guidance.

The man signaled to me that he had finished eating by no longer opening his mouth to receive the food. I noticed that his face had tensed up. He closed his eyes tightly and wrinkled his brow. He looked as though he was in intense pain. As I looked at his face I had an overwhelming urge to do something I'd never done before. I thought, "What I'm about to do may seem really weird," but my gut, my intuition, urged me to do it. I got up and leaned closer to him. I took the palm of my left hand and laid it across his forehead. In that instant his whole body melted into a relaxed state. From that furrowed brow all the way down to his feet, he simply relaxed. He seemed to let go of whatever pain he was holding or fighting against. He even let out a slight sigh of relief.

This man died the next day. All the patients I subsequently worked with died in different ways and for different medical reasons, but what was a constant, what was always the same, was the need for companionship, the need to be cared for, the unique human need not to die alone. What it really comes down to is compassion. Compassion is being with someone in their pain. There's a power in compassion, and it's very closely linked to the power of touch. For the sick and the elderly, those close to death, and especially those who are going through it alone, they have a real human need to be touched. When I was with that man I tried to empathize with his pain. It felt as though when I touched him, when I laid my hand across his forehead, some of his pain was relieved.

One thing I think I've come to understand about the process of death is the living, the people who are left behind. The people who are closest to the ones who die also need companionship and caring.

Death is uncomfortable to confront, and for those left behind we often have that same feeling of awkwardness, because we don't know what to do. When we know someone who has just lost a loved one we ask ourselves again and again, "What do I do? Should I send flowers, should I call, bring food?" I would say yes to all of the above; anything to let them know they're not alone. Sometimes the fear of doing the wrong thing in these situations causes people to do nothing at all, but what's most important is not worrying about getting it right. It's not about doing the right thing, it's about letting the ones who are left living know that they are not alone. Let them know you're thinking about them, that you're present with them. Even a small note speaks volumes.

No matter how small the gesture, acknowledging that there has been a loss lets the grieving person know that you're aware of the human condition, the painful feelings of sadness, the awareness that they've lost a piece of themselves. You are helping them to fill that void. I know this was true for me.

My sister, Ann, died at age 21 in a car crash. Her death was sudden and so completely unexpected. I think of her death, and all deaths that occur in this sudden fashion, as having the power to bring your life to a halt. Life seems to suddenly move in slow motion. The reason it felt that way to me was because the rest of the world just kept moving at its normal, hectic pace. I was left wondering how I was ever going to get back up to speed with life, because with Ann gone, it didn't seem like things could ever go back to normal.

For me, having the support of others and people to grieve with was what eventually brought me out of that slow-motion vortex. Friends who came to visit me didn't have to say a word in order to help me through my grief. Just their presence soothed me— just seeing someone I knew, I loved, who had come to be with me in that time that I call one of the most emotionally vulnerable moments in my life. There's something about that person's presence that brings about a different level of emotion; you know you're not alone in this pain and loss.

When people hear that I've volunteered with hospice, they frequently respond by saying, "Oh, I could never do that," or, "That takes a really special person." My response is always, "No, you could do it," and "No, there's nothing special about me." Volunteering for hospice does require getting over some fear and awkwardness, but anyone can do it. The most important aspect of the experience to me is that it provides companionship to people at the end of their lives, and anyone can be that companion.

Maybe that's why the man I was feeding relaxed and let go of whatever he was holding onto. When he felt my hand on his forehead, he knew he wasn't alone.

Making a U-Turn

F eeling so ashamed and so elated simultaneously doesn't seem like it could be humanly possible. These two feelings seem too counter-intuitive to occupy the same emotional space, yet as I whipped a U-turn, that's exactly the emotional state I was in.

As I recall, it was early May. There was a cold, hard rain falling, not yet that fun, refreshing, romantic summer rain. No, this was an uncomfortable rain, a rain that the windshield wipers can't keep up with, a blinding, cold, stinging rain...the kind that you want to end as soon as possible. I was driving to the airport and running late as usual. I suddenly noticed something very wrong. A woman was standing in this hellacious storm next to a sign that said, "Bus Stop." It was only the sign, no shelter, and no cover. The woman was holding what looked to be a small baby, maybe a few months old. I could see that she was holding the child as tightly as possible, huddled over it, trying to keep the baby dry. If this wasn't bad enough, there was another child maybe three years old; hiding between her legs, trying desperately to create some type of shelter from the cold rain.

I couldn't believe what I was seeing. Why in the world would this woman be standing outside in this weather? This unprepared mother, this irresponsible parent was exposing her children to such terrible conditions. How stupid could she be?

Then it hit me, like someone had just slugged me in the stomach so hard that I thought for a moment that I might throw up inside my car. The impact to my gut forced the thought to my mind: She needs shelter. She needs something to cover her and her children. Wait, I know. She needs what I have in the trunk of my car. She needs an umbrella.

Umbrella, what a beautiful word. It's a fun word to say when you think about it. Umbrella. It comes from the Latin root for umbra, meaning shade or shadow, and was invented over four thousand years ago. There's evidence of its use in artifacts from Egypt, Greece, and China. Now, on this spring day, its purpose is needed more than ever.

My eyes scanned the street for oncoming traffic. All clear. I looked behind me, it too was all clear. I hit my brakes and whipped a U-turn. Through the rain, I could see what looked to be an old driveway, but the house was no longer there. It was as close to her as I could get and still keep out of traffic, so I pulled in. From inside my car I opened the trunk. I grabbed my umbrella and started to run toward the woman through the rain. I felt so ashamed for having had all those judgmental thoughts about her. I didn't know why she had to stand in the rain that day. I didn't know her past or her present. All I knew was that she needed what I had in my hand. I was a few feet from her when I pushed the bottom on the umbrella handle. It made a whooshing sound as it opened outward, and the rain immediately started pelting off of my newfound shelter. I didn't remember it being so big; it seemed huge. When I reached her I couldn't look her in the eyes. I was too ashamed for having judged her so unfairly. I held it out, and with her free hand she took it from me. There were no words exchanged. I got back onto the road, realizing I was now running even later to catch my flight. I didn't really care though. By turning my car around, I had made a U-turn in my judgment as well and left it behind me. I felt redeemed from the negative thoughts that I had placed on this woman. Suddenly my destination didn't seem so important.

~

One cold January day I found myself once again making a split second decision to pull over on the side of the road. This time it was the person I stopped for who must have experienced that strange mixture of elation and shame. I had just turned onto Mount Hope road and was heading west when I saw someone hitchhiking. It was raining and about 38 degrees outside. This is a strange place to be looking for a ride. It's not in the city, but I think its close enough that the buses run on that road. So to be hitchhiking in this spot was odd. It's a narrow road with deep ditches on both sides, offering very little room to pull over. Judging on the basis of my own experience hitchhiking, I couldn't help but think how bad a spot this person had chosen to try to catch a ride. As I got closer, I couldn't tell if it was a young boy or a woman, however the face looked sad and desperate as if the eyes were pleading, "Please pick me up." To the chagrin of the travelers behind me, I slowed and only partially pulled off of the narrow road, making it difficult for others to pass me. The best I could do was pump my brakes to make sure they saw that I had stopped. When I checked my rearview mirror, the hitchhiker was already desperately running toward my car. I thought to myself, "What are you doing? This person could kill you!"

I also found myself worrying about what the other drivers

who were passing me thought about my decision. I imagined them thinking, "What kind of an idiot stops in this lane? What's he doing picking up a hitchhiker anyway?" I convinced myself to just let the thoughts pass and cleared the seat next to me.

The door opened. It was a woman about mid-thirties, 5' 2" with a small frame. Her brown and tan winter coat was large on her as well as being very dirty and stained. Her pants were the same, and she was wearing a knit stocking cap. She looked at me and started to cry. She had beautiful hands with long fingers that she spread over her eyes to hide the tears. Those hands struck me, maybe because of the way their elegance contrasted with her shabby clothes. "What happened? What's wrong?" I asked.

She told me she had turned a trick last night, and this guy took her to his home outside of town. She said he must have put something in her drink because the next thing she knew she woke up with him standing over her. He kicked her out of his house without paying her, telling her to walk home. Calling the police wasn't an option for her because what she was doing was illegal.

She wanted a ride to the west side of the city. As we drove she started telling me some of her story.

"I don't do this type of thing very often," she said, "but I needed to pay my electric bill by three o'clock today and now I have nothing. I had two jobs, but I just spent the last two weeks in the hospital because I have asthma really bad and they couldn't hold my jobs for me."

"Do you have kids?" I asked.

"I have two kids, a 22-year-old who's in prison and my sixteen-year-old girl, plus I have my grandchild, the child of my boy who's in prison." As we neared her neighborhood, she directed me to her street and told me to drop her at the corner, not pointing out a particular house. It occurred to me that she didn't want me to know exactly where she lived. It was a possible occupational hazard to give out that kind of information. She struck me as someone who had probably been burned in her life and didn't trust others easily.

As she was getting out of the car I asked her if she needed some money to get something to eat. I reached into my wallet and pulled out all the cash I had, which was about twelve dollars. She immediately said, "No, I can't take all your money." It made me feel sad that she thought that was all I had to my name, because I knew that must be how she lives; whatever you have on you is all the money you have. I explained to her that I had more money, that I could get more from my bank account, which convinced her to accept my offer. She thanked me for the ride and I drove away, stunned by this glimpse into her life. I wasn't left with the same sense of satisfaction that I had after giving an umbrella to the woman at the bus stop. The hitchhiker's problems seemed so vast that a ride home and twelve dollars wasn't going to do her much good. There's only so much one can do. I had done what I could; given her what I had to offer, but it wouldn't even come close to making a difference in her life. All I had done was provide a fleeting moment of comfort.

~

Chic Broersma was the campus minister when I was in school at Grand Valley State University. He was the first person I had ever met who really exemplified what Christianity is supposed to be about. He was non-judgmental, open-minded, and accepting of you as a person, just the way you are. One day, Chic was on his way into the library when we crossed paths and exchanged greetings. He asked me how I was doing and I decided to be honest.

"Not so good." He asked me if I wanted to talk about it. I politely declined, saying that I didn't want to get in the way of whatever he was planning to do at the library. "The library will always be there," he told me. "Why don't we go for a walk and have a talk."

I was stunned that he stopped everything and paid attention to me. I felt valued. I was important enough for someone to drop what they were doing to help me out. At the time there were probably lots of things that needed fixing in my life, but Chic didn't need to attend to all of them. In this case, all he did was listen. He made a "U-turn" and just gave me what he had—his time.

It's natural to want to "fix" a person's problems, but for someone like the hitchhiker, no amount of money could repair her life. You can fix a bike, but human problems are much more complex. What we can do, however, is make that U-turn, re-route our direction, hit the pause button on our own concerns, and stop to give someone what we can. Those small gestures won't "fix" a person's life, but they can make a difference. Any moment when we are able to make someone feel that they're not alone, no matter how fleeting, has value.

Can you think of a time in your life when someone did this for you, when someone noticed that you were in need and took the time to help? I wonder if experiences where I've received the charity of others, like when Chic took the time to talk with me, somehow led to me pulling my car over, changing my direction, and scanning myself for what I had to give. Perhaps doing this was my small way of passing on what others had given me.

People who need help won't always be as obvious as a mother and her children standing in the rain. But when we do see someone in need, we can slow down, look both ways, check the trunk, and make a U-turn.

Invisible

Have you ever had someone you don't know start talking to you and assume that you know exactly what they're talking about? Well, that's what happened....

After I had performed a show at a fundraiser, a guy in his late thirties, medium build, approached me. His face and body language cried out hesitation and shyness, yet an eagerness to connect with me. He waited around until everyone was gone. He stepped up and said,

"Who told you?"

"Who told me what?" I said.

"Did they tell you about me?" He asked.

"I'm sorry, but I don't know what you're talking about," I said.

The guy paused, looking at me with an inquisitive look, like puppies when they tilt their heads trying to figure out what it is you want from them.

"You told that story about me, but you just changed my name," he said.

"What story did I tell about you? I don't know you," I said.

By this time, a minute of total confusion has passed. I really didn't have a clue what this guy was talking about. I was beginning to think he'd missed his meds and had mistaken me for someone else.

"What story are you talking about?" I asked

"The story about Bill," he said. "That was me." The story I told that night during my talk was about a student named Bill. It so closely mirrored this man's own experience that he thought I was talking about him. I was taken aback, because by identifying with Bill, this man standing in front of me had just confessed to a personal history of loneliness and isolation.

I met the real Bill at a weekend retreat for high school students called Partners in Prevention (PIP). PIP, also called a lock-out, was basically a weekend retreat about drug prevention and ways to live a healthy lifestyle. The lock-out symbolizes locking out the troubles of the world in order to focus on what really mat- ters...personal development. PIP usually started on Friday night and ended Sunday at noon. Students from a hundred mile radius converged on a local high school where we had large group pre- sentations on a variety of topics. Then students would break into smaller groups to process the information. I was an adult leader of a small group.

For the most part, all had gone well during our small group. We were wrapping up our last meeting, talking about what it would be like to go back to our lives again on Monday, and how we would talk about what had happened here. That's when this student named Bill spoke for the first time.

I had noticed during the retreat that outside our small group, Bill was usually by himself. When I did try to engage him, it was hard for him to converse. Bill was a senior, three months from graduation, and yet I could tell he wasn't used to carrying on a normal teen conversation or interacting with people. He was your classic loner. Although the students were encouraged to share, talking about personal issues was optional. Bill had chosen not to talk thus far. As we sat in our small group circle on the floor, talking about the people with whom we would share this experience, he said with hesitation, "I'm going to tell my friend about this weekend."

"That's great. Is your friend a senior, too?" I asked.

"No, he's not."

"Oh. Is he a junior?"

"No."

"Freshman? Sophomore?"

"No." Now I'm getting worried. I just opened a can of worms that I didn't want to open this late in the game. I asked, "Is your friend a teacher?"

"No." Bill said. Now I'm thinking to myself, "Here we go, his friend is some type of invisible friend or space alien or something really strange, and I'm going to help expose his dysfunction in front of our small group." I felt the need to be honest and get clarification for all of us on what he was talking about, so I asked, "I give up Bill, who's your friend?"

Bill stumbled over his words, struggling to expose the embarrassing truth. "He's the custodian." We all paused in silence. The girl just to my right started to cry and then another girl. Then Bill began to cry and soon we were all crying about the truth of Bill. He was attending a school with a population of nine hundred students, and the only friend he had was the custodian. I asked our group," Do you know why we're crying?" The students looked at me with sad, wet checks and shook their heads. I said, "Because you know how painful, lonely, and sad it would be. That's why we're crying."

As we dried our tears a question occurred to me. I'm still not sure where this question came from. Whatever the source, I asked him, "Bill, do you ever go to the school dances?" He looked at me and seemed to perk up a bit, saying, "My grandmother gave me her car, so yeah, I do go to the dances." He seemed pleased to have answered this question, proud that he had the use of a car, I suppose.

"Bill, have you ever danced with anyone?" I asked.

"No."

"What do you do at the dances, Bill?"

"I just stand along the wall and watch the others dance."

~

The man who came up to me after my talk clearly still identified Bill with the person he was in high school. He was a grown man now, and he was still so tied to that image of himself that he actually thought I was talking about him. "Who told you about me?" he had said.

"So, you were a Bill?" I said to the man standing in front of me with the sad eyes.

"Yes," he said, "but instead of standing along the wall, I stood behind a wood lattice fence with plastic plants hanging from it. They put the fence on the stage in the gym for decoration. I stood behind it watching the dance through the holes in the fence."

"What did you need?" I asked him. "What would have made a difference for you? How could someone have helped you come out from behind the fence?"

"I just needed someone to notice me. It was as if I was invisible, and I didn't know how to make my self appear."

At times everyone feels lonely. With roughly seven billion of us on this planet flying through space, we can be so alone. Throughout history, scientists in the fields of sociology, psychology, and anthropology have agreed that humans are social creatures. We function best when we're with other people. In my research on loneliness and happiness, after the lab lights are turned off and the experiments are over, the experts say that we're connected to each other. We belong to each other. We're made for each other. Life is a journey through time, and happiness is what happens when we make that journey together. Basically we need other humans in our lives. That's it!

I find that there's feeling lonely, and there's being alone without others in our lives. Some people are pretty much fine with being alone—they live it, they choose it. However, I know people who feel lonely, who do not have others in their lives, and they don't choose to be that way. They just can't seem to change it.

That day at the lock-out, the students in our small group gave Bill lots of ideas on how to make friends, but my hunch is that he would not be able to implement them on his own. He needed help. He needed someone to reach out to him. He needed to be asked to dance; otherwise he would do what he knows how to do...stand against the wall and watch.

Our need for others is so powerful; it's such a natural, normal part of being human. We know this to be true because if we really want to be mean to someone and teach them a lesson, we will deliberately put them in isolation.

We sometimes start this treatment of others at a very early age. "Time Out" for a toddler is removing them from the pack, letting them know what it feels like to be alone, to feel lonely. They come back waving the white flag, crying, "Ok, I got it! I'll stop throwing my Cheerios on the floor."

We take this concept to the next level with adults in our prison system. If you're sentenced to a life term in prison, how do they get you to obey the rules? They've already locked you up so they can't do that again. But what they can do is put you in isolation, "the hole" as it's referred to. Certain bad behaviors will earn an inmate a ticket, and after a certain amount of tickets or points the prisoner spends time in a small, sometimes windowless cell, with no human contact. And if the crimes and behaviors are deemed anti-social enough, inmates are placed in permanent solitary confinement, sometimes going decades of their lives without any real human interaction. Aside from the death penalty, placing someone in isolation, forcing them to feel lonely is the highest form of punishment our society can inflict. Experts say that when you are lonely your whole body is lonely. Loneliness even affects the basic functions of the human body.

It's estimated that 20% of the United States population, about 60 million people, suffer from loneliness. Walk on any high school or college campus, and if a person is alone, it seems they have their cell phone to their ear, are reading emails, or have headphones on, listening to anything but a real human. What's missing are people connecting human to human—a look, a nod, saying "Hi". Technology has created a barrier against this very human need and natural desire to connect, making it nearly impossible. You may be connected by a piece of hardware, but you're not truly emotionally connected.

In the jumbo, mega-hit movie, *Avatar*, the tribe Na'vi has a tradition of keeping loneliness at bay by simply saying, "I see you," when they meet, because if just one other sees you, you'll never be alone.

Loneliness can be hard to detect in others. It doesn't have an outer appearance, per se. You can't look at someone and tell whether they are lonely or not. It's not like a physical disability that's visible in someone's body, but it can be just as debilitating. There are people all around us who are invisible and live their lives in isolation. If we look close enough we'll see the person standing against the wall or the eyes behind the fence. Just acknowledging that person, showing them that "I see you," can dissolve some of that loneliness.

III.
WISDOM COMES FROM UNEXPECTED PLACES

Memorizing
the Darkness

Aquinas College in Grand Rapids, Michigan asked me to do a talk for 400 incoming freshmen at the onset of the fall semester. The goal of my program was to help prepare them for the new educational journey they were embarking on and to pass on a little advice.

I opened my talk with some general observations, one of which was a half page article in the *Grand Rapids Press* about their class doing volunteer work in the community. I then turned the focus on myself; I know that for me, entering college was difficult, scary and overwhelming. I was excited for the opportunity to share my experience with these students, and hopefully provide them with some tools to navigate the bumpy terrain of college life. It was a great group of students with good energy in the room. I felt I had a solid program, some big laughs, and some nice silent, meaningful moments. I didn't expect, however, the true, profound, and teachable moments to occur after my talk was over.

As I wrapped up my goodbyes and exited the building, I saw

a group of about fifteen students standing in a circle under the shade of a large oak, receiving directions from their orientation leader. For those of you who went to college, you know what these leaders are like, often wearing an oversized name tag with smiley faces stuck to it around their neck and greeting new students with an overly enthusiastic and unrealistic attitude about the glories of college life. I looked at the group and thought to myself, "Eh... why not?" I walked up and said, "What's up?" They all seemed to react enthusiastically when they saw it was me, the "speaker guy." I caught them off guard. They were surprised to see me, but they seemed genuinely pleased. They said all the right stuff: "You were great." "You're really funny." "We loved your program."

I thanked them and told them that they were a great group to perform for, then asked, "Hey, I was wondering if there was anything in my talk that was especially meaningful to you?" Organizations often give surveys to my audiences after my talks to get feedback. In this case the college hadn't done so, and I was eager to see what their off-the-cuff reaction would be...a little peek into the mind of a college freshman. Instantly a young blonde woman with an innocent smile said, "I really liked it when you talked about your wife and family." I was taken aback, thinking to myself, "I did?" The topic of my talk certainly wasn't about marriage and family. I must have mentioned things about my wife and kids without even realizing I was doing it. "Why did you like that part?" I asked her.

"Because you're still married, and you seem happy. Most of our parents are divorced. It's just good to see that it can work out."

Most of the group concurred. I was truly surprised by her comment and the agreement among the group. It makes sense to me now that I think about it. Most specialists in the fields of anthropology and cellular biology believe that the desire to find a partner can be traced back to a biological determinant, an evolutionary instinct that drives the desire to have our genes carried on in the next generation. Surviving a marriage and having a family seemed so far away from the message I had just delivered, but it occurred to me that behind the concerns of weekend keggers and final exams, college students are largely preoccupied with the question of when and how they will find a mate. Not a date, but a mate...someone to spend your life with, have children with, and hopefully live happily ever after.

As though to prove the frequency of divorce in the students' lives, a young man to my left piped in, "Hey, my parents just got divorced two weeks ago." I could tell that everyone in the group just heard this personal information for the first time, and we were all overwhelmed with the sadness of his tone.

"Wow, that's good timing," I replied. "Just as you're leaving for college, you're taking a big step in life. And, now this?"

"Yeah, tell me about it!" he said.

"So, at your first break from school," I asked him, "do you know where home is, where you will go?"

He shook his head and said, "No, not really." I let that thought sink in, hang for a few moments, and then I noticed a girl holding a walking cane. It was the long white kind with the red tip that's used by the visually impaired. I was curious about her level of sight so I asked,

"Who's this person with the walking cane?"

"Are you talking about me?" she said.

"Well, you probably can't see it, but you're the only one in the group with a cane. Can you see shadows, or can you see the difference between light and darkness?" She didn't even pause before shooting back at me,

"My eye balls aren't even real. I could take them out and throw them at you." The whole group, including myself, was shocked. I thought, "Wow! This girl has some spunk!"

"How are you going to hit me if you can't see me?" I asked.

"I have a really good sense of space. I'll hit you!" We all laughed. It was one of those 'Thank God we can all laugh' moments, and we certainly needed one of those. I'm thinking, "Who is this blind girl with such chutzpah, and what is her story?" Thinking back on what she said about her sense of space, I pictured her as a young Jedi warrior, using her cane like a light saber, calling on the force to tell her where I am so she can strike me down.

"What caused you to lose your real eyes?" I asked. She told us that when she was a little girl she was diagnosed with retinal cancer, and they gave her two choices. She could either keep her eyes and die, or lose her sight and live. Everyone standing in our group was genuinely in awe of the childhood trauma that she was revealing to us. We were amazed by her frankness and honesty about it all. Thus far, all they knew was that she walked with a cane. It probably never occurred to them that she might not have been born blind, that she had vision at one point and something happened to take that away from her. I asked her how she was going to get around campus. She pointed to the girl next to her and said, "Anna is going to help me memorize the campus for the next two weeks. Then I'll be able to get where I need to go on my own. I've been doing it for a long time now. I'm pretty good at it."

When I think of things I'm good at, I think of riding my bike, running, and balancing a broom stick on my finger. She, on the other hand, is pretty good at walking into the unknown every day and memorizing the dark, empty space around her. She's good at being able to ask for the help she needs when starting something new or encountering a strange environment. It turns out that she's also good at reminding me, and perhaps others, to take the next step into the unknown, keep moving, and ask for the help we need along the way. This is a lesson I've learned time and again—that asking for help when approaching new and unknown situations is much easier and less frightening than trying to go it alone.

I found her to be an inspiring young woman with an incredible story of perseverance. As I was saying goodbye to the group I asked her, "If I walk up to you this year on campus and say, 'Hi,' will you remember my voice?" She paused for effect, and said with an all-knowing attitude, "Oh yeah, I'll remember you."

Isabel's Five Ideas

One afternoon I was feeling lonely, melancholy, a little down. I was preparing to give a talk and couldn't shake these feelings. How do you inspire and teach others when you feel down?

In my early career as a speaker, I struggled with the idea that the advice I gave people during my talks had to match perfectly with the actions I took in my own life. I was so concerned with being inauthentic that I beat myself up over any misstep and the inability to live up to my full potential in life. Eventually I learned that this goal is impossible. Everyone has ups and downs in their life, and my own don't make me unfit to try to inspire others. They just make me human. However, at this time I was a young father and husband, early in my career, and I hadn't learned this yet. One phrase that helped me get over this was, "We teach what we need to learn the most." Sometimes I tell groups, "You really need to be cautious of people like me. Am I teaching you what you need to learn, or am I saying things that I need to teach myself?" One thing that I've always found to be true, though, is that if you're ever looking for true authenticity, ask a child.

I was folding clothes on our bed, and Isabel, my almost five year old daughter at the time, wandered into our bedroom, jumped up on the bed, and just looked at me.

In a flash of insight I thought to myself, "Maybe she has some ideas of what I should tell people that would be meaningful to them, because at the moment I feel empty."

"Isabel," I said, "what do you think would be five things I should tell people? What are five things you think people should know?"

She hesitated for all of two seconds and then said with a very adult posture, "Well, tell people that God loves them in their heart." I didn't expect her to bring God into this. I thought about it for a moment and asked her, "What do you mean; he loves us in our heart?"

She said, "Daddy, your spirit is in your heart, and God gave you his spirit, so he loves your heart." This came out with a tone of "Hey you idiot, everybody knows that!"

"Ok," I said, feeling like a fool. "What's the second thing I should tell people?"

"Tell them about me and Malcolm."

"Why?" I asked.

"Because I'm your daughter and Malcolm is your son, and you should tell people about us."

I thought, "Wow! I should be doing a little PR for my kids?" I said, "Ok, that's fair. I'll tell people about you. What's number three?"

Without hesitation she said, "Tell people to be happy because they will *get* presents and they will *give* presents." What I loved about this is that she didn't say "should," that people "should" be happy. She just wanted me to tell them, "be happy," like happiness is right at your fingertips—you just have to receive it and share your gifts with others. It's something along the lines of that "better to give than receive" idea.

This one really struck me as having a sense of abstract sophistication. I told her to hold on, I'll be right back. I literally ran to my office, grabbed a pen and paper, brought it back into our bedroom, and wrote down the first three ideas. After writing them down I checked with Isabel to make sure that I'd gotten the first three correct. I had. I'm now prepared to write. "Ok, Isabel, what's the fourth one?"

Isabel thought for a few seconds and then said, "Tell people they will have children and babies, or you don't have to. You can have fun both ways."

I asked again, making sure I had heard her correctly. "What did you just say?" She repeated back the exact same thought. I'm thinking to myself, "I don't know if I can share that one. People are going to think there's something really weird going on in our house." But I wrote it down. It was one of her ideas.

Finally, the fifth and final idea. "What's number five?" I asked.

With all sincerity and quite a serious tone she said, "Tell them that they're never really alone. God will be with them every day."

I almost started to cry on the spot. Even now, ten years later, I become emotional just thinking about it. She had no idea how much I needed to hear those words. It was as if God wanted me to be sad and lonely that day so I would stop my life and ask an almost five year old what I should tell other people, when really I was the one who needed to hear her five ideas.

As I write this she is now almost sixteen. I've shared her ideas with groups periodically, and inevitably there are people who come up to me after the presentation to share how one or more of those ideas has touched them.

A few pieces of feedback that people have shared with me about Isabel's five ideas:

Number 1: Some people live in their heads, and some people live in their hearts. I think this one particularly struck me because she reminded me that that's where God put our spirit, our soul. He put it in our heart, and that's the place I need to look to for guidance. I was in my head. She brought me back to my heart.

Number 2: We should talk about the people we love in our lives. Why not?

Number 3: After hearing this, Ted Klontz, a good friend and psychologist, said that one of the greatest gifts you can give anyone is to just be present with them.

Number 4: The wild card. I've had women who could not conceive children thank me for sharing this, and I've had nuns who have told me, "Your daughter is right. All the babies of the world are mine to care for."

As for Number 5: I'm not sure when she became a theologian or when she attended Bible Study. How did she know what she knew?

Many philosophers from Buddhists to Christians have spoken of the beauty and wisdom of a child's mind. Jesus said, "Let the children come to me. Don't stop them! For the Kingdom of Heaven belongs to those who are like these children."

At that time in my life I was preoccupied with the concept of authenticity, but Isabel wasn't. It would never occur to her young mind to question whether what she thought was true. She spoke from her heart, all the time.

As adults, we have our moments of being sad, overwhelmed, depressed and lost. When we feel this way, attaining peace and happiness can seem like a distant possibility. But, I truly believe that in times of despair, if we think about the things that Isabel said we can feel that peace of mind is just as simple and attainable as she saw it. Remember the simplicity. I was searching for direction outside of myself, and this almost five year old reminded me to go back to my spirit, on the inside, for the answers I needed.

Keep Dreaming

The concierge directed me towards a pharmacy about ten blocks from our hotel. I had just arrived in San Jose, California and brought with me a severe sinus infection. I was feeling sick as a dog. My doctor had called in a prescription to knock out the virus. I needed to start it right away. I took a taxi to the pharmacy, picked up my meds, and bought a bottle of juice to wash them down. As I walked outside to hail a taxi back to the hotel, I suddenly felt the warm sun on my face and decided that it'd be a shame to waste the beautiful weather. It was the middle of January. When I left Michigan there was two feet of snow on the ground with a temperature of negative ten degrees. I hadn't seen the sun in months or felt warmth for even longer. I'd been hiding like a gnome, hunkering down for the Michigan winter. So, as you can imagine, the warmth and walk offered a welcome change of scenery.

I began my stroll, and when I was about four blocks from my hotel, I came upon a tree full of oranges. What a bright embodiment of sunny California...*an orange tree*! The brightly colored fruit hung like ornaments on a Christmas tree. I stopped for a moment to take in this image. As I stood admiring the foliage I heard someone, or some *thing* say, "Hi," but I couldn't make out where it was coming from. Again I heard it. "Hi."

I started to wonder, "What kind of pill did I take?" Now thinking that the oranges were talking to me I was about to say, "Hi" back when I heard a voice behind me saying, "Over here."

I turned to see a man and a woman sitting on the front lawn of a church that I hadn't even noticed until this moment.

He asked me, "You're not from here, are you?"

"No," I answered, "I just got in today. Hey, did you know you have oranges?"

"Yes. We know. We live here."

"You fool!" I thought to myself. "They're sitting on this lawn eating lunch out of white plastic bags, looking right at this orange tree—I think they must know."

I walked over to introduce myself. His name was Mike and his wife's name was Lori. We chatted for a short time. I told them I was here to speak at a state-wide youth conference being held at my hotel. Picking up on my appreciation for California's beauty, Mike informed me of a beautiful park just across the street where I could see a variety of different species of plants and birds that I wouldn't see back in Michigan. He struck me as possessing an above average knowledge of botany and wildlife. I thanked him for the heads-up and was about ready to walk off when it occurred to me that I had neglected to ask Mike one of the most commonly asked questions in the world:

"What do you do?"

In our society, in the U.S. especially, we ask this question all the time. On a plane when you talk with the person next to you, often you won't even ask the person's name, but you will ask what their occupation is. There are all kinds of judgments that go along with this question. Based on the answer, we tend to put people in a box, mentally place them in a hierarchy of social status. We can estimate about how much money they make, their level of education, their lifestyle, what kind of house they live in and vacations they take.

When I posed this question to Mike, "What do you do?" I expected something basic, but also something that could be very "California" and hip. I certainly didn't expect the answer I received.

"I'm homeless."

I was shocked, speechless, and honestly, I was a little suspicious. My initial thought was, "This is a scam. Now I know why he's being so nice to me." I felt like I'd been taken and braced myself for his next move, which I assumed would be to ask me for money. To try to catch him off guard, and judge whether he was being honest with me about his living situation, I asked him,

"You're homeless? So where did you stay last night?"

"My wife and I spent the last two nights at a friend's apartment. He's away."

"Well, where will you stay tonight?" I asked, still suspicious.

Without hesitation or embarrassment he answered matter-of-factly, "Probably in a shelter." That's when I knew he was being genuine.

After that exchange we talked some more about his life and current situation. I was impressed with his gentle demeanor and the way in which he carried himself. He didn't fit the typical conception of what a homeless person is like. I sensed that he might have a unique perspective on life; maybe some insights that I could share with others.

I said, "Mike, I'm speaking to seven hundred 9th through 12th graders tonight. If you could tell them anything, what would you say?"

I could tell he was flattered and humbled by the idea. "I wouldn't have anything to say to them," he said.

"No." I said, "As a homeless man, what have you learned that you could share with seven hundred high school students to make a difference in their lives?" I could tell that this made him think... the idea that he could make a difference in people's lives.

Mike paused and said, "Okay, just off the top...from my heart."

He brought his hands up to each side of his face, held them to the outside of his eyes, like blinders on a racehorse, and said,

"I would tell them to stay focused, and don't let anyone take you from your dreams."

"Is that what happened to you?" I asked.

He looked at me, nodding his head in agreement. I put my hand out and he grabbed it, holding on firmly. I assured him,

"I'll tell them."

While walking the remaining few blocks back to my hotel, I glanced down a side street and saw a line of people standing outside a shelter, being handed white plastic bags, the same bags that Mike and Lori were eating from. If I needed any more proof that Mike was presenting a genuine picture of his life, that was it. That night I told the kids at the conference what Mike had said. "Don't let anyone take you from your dreams."

When we're preparing high schoolers for adult life, we look at their grades, areas of strength and weakness, how much money they'd like to make at their future job, and what kind of higher education or training they should pursue to get them there. We rarely ask what their *dreams* are. I know that when I was in high school, I thought that if I had a good job and made lots of money I'd be happy. I think that mindset is prevalent in people of all ages. However, all the research shows that money can't buy you happiness. Even when people do try to focus on their dreams, they often aren't able to see a dream as being anything other than an occupation. We ask, "What's your dream job?"—still having a hard time separating personal aspirations from that narrow path of a *job*. But if we're truly getting into the realm of fantasy, dreams go beyond a job. They go to ideas of purpose, passion, and creativity.

When I asked Mike to offer his thoughts to high schoolers, he didn't advise them to stay off drugs, stay in school, or be careful with their money. Off the top of his head from his heart, he spoke about dreams, because they ultimately trump the typical preventative advice of, "Don't do this. Don't do that." Instead Mike's advice suggests saying "yes" to something; finding a solution that promises far more fulfillment than chasing money.

To this day I believe that Mike is one of the better teachers I've encountered. I don't think about it every day, but sometimes when I see a homeless person I wonder what their dream was. I know that when they were in school, they didn't sit behind a desk thinking to themselves, "Someday I'll live on the streets, be poor, and struggle just to survive day to day." No, they had a dream. They saw themselves as happy, loving, and enjoying life, just like me. I saw a video once of the Dali Lama being interviewed about diversity issues. He said, "When you see someone else, they're another you. They have passions and dreams; and they want to love and be loved just like you."

No Words

When I was nineteen being a 'ski bum' seemed like a great way to hang out. A former high school classmate, Richard, and I had stayed in touch and talked about someday going out West and getting jobs at a ski resort. This idea seemed exotic and wild to us. About a year after high school graduation, the day finally came for us to embark on the adventure we'd been dreaming of for a number of years. I knew that during this year of experimental living I would learn many things and encounter many new experiences. But I couldn't have predicted that my new life would involve learning about the world of the deaf.

At the last minute, Richard invited his friend Ricky to come along with us on our odyssey. Ricky could neither hear nor speak; he was a person who used to be referred to as a deaf-mute.

Growing up on a farm, I had never met a deaf person or anyone who couldn't speak. My lack of knowledge about the deaf was so extreme that I was under the impression people with these impairments were also mentally impaired. Getting to know Ricky turned these notions on their head and opened my mind to realizing just how capable he was. I was soon to discover how brilliant a guy he was.

Our plan was to drive to Colorado in Richard's robin-egg blue, Chevy van that was tricked out on the inside with floor to ceiling shag carpet. Normally on a long road trip like this, whether with your friends or someone new, you use it as an opportunity to get to know each other better by talking the whole way. This wasn't going to be an option for Ricky and me. It was my first experience hanging out with someone who couldn't talk or hear, and there I was, stuck in a van with Ricky for seventeen hours, him not speaking vocally, and me obviously not knowing sign language.

I was nervous about the awkwardness of the situation that I would be in over the course of a two-day drive. I was puzzled at how this would work. I was afraid that there would be lots of uncomfortable quiet time between Ricky and me. This awkwardness caused me to imagine all kinds of extreme scenarios that might occur as a result of our inability to communicate. For example, during our first stop for lunch at a chicken shack, it occurred to me that if Richard left the room and Ricky started choking on a chicken bone, I wouldn't have any way of knowing. This whole no talking, no hearing thing really limits one's ability to build a relationship. Not to mention saving someone from choking on a chicken bone. Of course this was an irrational thought because the gesture used to indicate choking is universally understood. You put your hands around your neck and gag. And besides, a person who can speak wouldn't be able to tell you with words that they're choking any more than Ricky could.

During the trip, I slowly discovered ways of communicating with Ricky. We were able to relay simple ideas to one another. I found myself performing lots of pantomiming and asking Richard, who could sign, to translate our questions and answers.

Have you ever spent time with a person who is deaf or is unable to speak? I don't mean just hard of hearing; I'm talking about a person who cannot hear anything. If they're really good lip readers it makes a huge difference in your ability to carry on some type of conversation. But, if you don't sign, or they don't read lips, plan B is a game of charades. When we initially attempted to exchange ideas I would act out everything I wanted to say, and then wait for one of three responses. Ricky would answer my pantomimes by either nodding his head up and down for 'yes', or shaking his head from side to side for 'no'. The third and most common response would be for him to shrug his shoulders and lift his hands in the air with palms facing upward, with a face to match that says loud and clear, "What the heck are you talking about?"

Assuming you don't sign, think about some basic idea, a thought you'd want to relay to a deaf person. Let's say you wanted to ask them, "How are you feeling today?" How would you act that out? What would you do with your hands? How would you use your body to communicate that question? How would you even communicate that what you're saying to them *is* a question?

At first this new way of translating your thoughts to someone that you don't know is maddening. You'll find yourself doing lots of pointing and mouthing words with exaggerated facial movements, and instinctively employing the irrational technique of speaking really loudly, much in the same way that we find ourselves doing with people who speak a foreign language. I'm certainly not the first person to feel inadequate when encountering someone who can't hear me. Misconceptions about the hearing impaired date at least as far back as the time of Aristotle, who thought that only people who can hear the spoken word could learn. Deaf people at that time were thought to be incapable of reasoned thinking and therefore unable to be educated.

In my time with Ricky I quickly realized that not only was he a fantastic, wonderful guy, but he was also one of the most brilliant men I'd ever met. His intelligence was especially apparent when it came to small, hand manipulated puzzles like the Rubik's Cube and other tricky mind bending games that I couldn't even begin to solve. His ability to focus was amazing. He could look at any puzzle and hand it back completely figured out in a matter of minutes.

Despite Ricky's many abilities there was one instance when his inability to hear almost got him killed. We were driving in the mountains on secondary roads, which are especially treacherous, very narrow, and full of switchbacks. We came upon a few cars that had hit some black ice and spun out, blocking the road. We pulled over and started pushing cars that had skidded on the ice, eventually clearing the small traffic jam so we could get moving again. Richard was back in the van, and just as I was stepping through the back sliding door, I heard a car horn blaring, the way that people only lay on the horn when something is very wrong.

I whipped my head around to see Ricky walking back across the icy road toward the van. He didn't hear the horn or see the car coming at him. The unsuspecting vehicle had rounded the corner, not prepared for a sheet of ice, and definitely not prepared for a person standing in the middle of the road. I instinctively yelled out to Ricky and just as quickly remembered that he couldn't hear me. I pointed wildly as if a tiger was coming at him. He turned just in time to put his hands on the front grill of the car. We watched in awe as Ricky was being pushed backwards, his shoes sliding on the ice. It looked as if he was superman stopping a speeding train, and after sliding for about fifty feet, both Ricky and the car finally came to a stop. Immediately the driver's door flew open wide. Out stepped a large intimidating man with a voice that matched his size. Pointing his finger at Ricky he yelled, "Are you crazy? What are you doing?" Richard and I then yelled at 'big angry man,' "He's deaf! He can't hear you!" The man, distracted by the chaos, did not hear or see another car coming around the same curve. It too tried stopping, but thanks to the black ice, lost control and crashed into the door 'angry man' left open. Ricky looked at us with raised eyebrows, then back at the cars, looked at us again, and wiped his brow in an exaggerated motion. "Oh, I get it," He was saying, "Phew, that was close. I was almost killed." I thought to myself, "Hey, I do know sign language!" Ricky jumped into the van, and we sped away. Some experiences need no words.

IV.
TRUSTING
YOUR INSTINCTS

Butterflies
Behind Bars

I've read a lot of newspapers and magazines, many articles that caught my attention and made me think, but only once did a morning's reading cause me to wind up in prison. The article in question presented some staggering statistics about the crime rate among inner city teens. It wasn't exactly a new topic, but seeing the numbers on paper jarred me and opened up something in my thinking.

The idea hit me like a rock falling from the ceiling, setting off an inner voice that said, "Go meet the statistics!" The voice was so strong that I felt an immediate need to obey. I put down the paper I was reading and called my mother. She would know how to meet the statistics. She spent over 20 years in prisons, and no, not because she killed our babysitters. She worked as a nurse to the inmates. She could advise me on how to get in and get back out again without getting hurt. I told her my idea of going to meet these young criminals to investigate what happened to cause them to be incarcerated. That's what the inner voice was telling me to do. Go meet these guys. Ask them what went wrong, starting from their childhood. I wanted to learn about their lives, uncover the stories behind the statistics. I was sick of reading about our prisons filling up with youth. At the time I was working directly with children in schools, and my idealistic hope was that if I spoke one-on-one with these men I might find some insight, and that insight might lead to preventative measures that I could share with the students who still had a chance at a good life.

I discovered a prison in Ionia, Michigan that held 17 to 20 year olds. It was a temporary holding facility that's referred to as "quarantine." This place is where prisoners waited between six to eight weeks before being sent to what would eventually be their home for two years to life. It all depended on the type of crime they had committed. I did the needed paperwork and met with the warden, who then introduced me to a prison psychologist. I was going to use her office on the inside to conduct my interviews.

I was extremely unnerved going in the first time, filled with fear about entering this unknown world. I worried that the inmates would yell at me or even hurt me physically. I was concerned that they might resent me probing into their lives and that they might react with anger.

Anyone going to the inside, gaining direct access to the prisoners, has to go through what's called the "Bubble." In this prison, the Bubble was a small 5 by 5 foot glass and steel room. You step in, and the door slides closed behind you. The Bubble is operated by a guard who sits on the other side of the glass, in a separate room. Anyone entering or leaving the prison is seen by him. I would stand there for a few moments while he looked me over, holding my bag with a tape recorder and notepad that had already been riffled through by prison security. My first time going through this process, while standing there being scrutinized, I was flooded with a sudden paranoia. I did a quick mental scan, asking myself, "Have I done anything illegal that they could know about? Is there any contraband on me that would give them an excuse to keep me behind these doors?" After you've been looked over and cleared, the door on the other side opens. You walk through that door and BANG, the heavy steel slams behind you, lightening fast and with a loud crash that leaves you with a sense of finality, like there's no going back. Now you're on the inside. You don't get to leave until the guard operating the Bubble releases you back to the outside world. The closing of those heavy doors was a sound that echoed through the halls of the prison constantly. Bang. Bang. Bang. Always doors banging shut all around you. Sometimes I thought it would be funny to shout out, "People, can we stop slamming doors please?" But, I didn't feel like getting shanked so I kept my mouth shut.

The flyer that was posted for the prisoners to read said, "Wanted: Interviews of your life story. What can others learn from you in order for them to live a better life? Sign up now."

I had more guys sign up on the first day than I needed to interview for the entire project. Apparently they all wanted to tell their story. I think everyone wants to tell their story. It's a way of having your life matter, and someone has to listen in order for it to count.

The interview room was small with thick steel bars on one small window. It was mostly bare and always cold. There was a metal desk and two metal chairs with minimum padding. I knew I couldn't write fast enough to keep up with the conversations, so I put my cassette recorder on the desk in plain sight. I figured that when they saw the recorder they may change their minds, but no one did.

I had a very deliberate strategy going into my initial meeting with the inmates. My ritual was to stand up and greet the prisoner with a solid look in the eye and a firm handshake. I felt there was a lot riding on the first impression. In that one initial exchange of shaking hands and making eye contact I was trying to make them feel welcome and respected, and at the same time communicate a sense of seriousness and purpose. I pretended to know what I was doing in my role as interviewer. I knew I had to get these first interviews right in order to gain their respect. I could tell they were very leery of me, and I couldn't blame them. I didn't really trust myself yet either. Remember, this is prison. It's a different world. Gossip and intel travels faster on the inside than in the outside world. There was still no intel on me...no word yet on whether I was for real or not, so this first interview needed to go well. My strategy was to "come clean." My mother had warned me that these guys are pros at reading people, so just tell them the truth.

Thus, I started by telling them, "Look, I grew up on a farm, one of ten kids, did poorly in school, but made it to college. I'm a speaker. I talk to people about life and maybe how they can make their lives better. I don't know what it's like to grow up in the city, be part of a gang, deal drugs, walk around with a gun, or come from poverty. That's why I'm here. You tell me, and I'll share your story with the outside world." This usually brought a smile to their faces. They were in the power seat. They were the teacher. With that we were on our way. The biggest shocker for these guys was the fact that I really wanted them to just talk about themselves. This seemed to be the largest hurdle to get over. They were amazed because no one had ever really asked this of them before.

Here are some of their stories:

JJ's father died when he was about 12. He loved his dad. They went fishing, played catch, did all the things dads do with their sons. After his father's death, he said no one really understood his pain and how sad he was. He felt like he couldn't really trust anyone any more. His downward spiral started with fighting with his mother, then a mean stepfather. That escalated into getting into trouble at school and eventually getting kicked out, hanging with the wrong kids, getting high, drinking, and finally joining a gang...all the things he knew his dad would not have approved of. He's now serving 24 years for shooting a guy in the back. The man he shot was a rival gang member who disrespected him. He seemed quite confident that none of this would have happened if someone had intervened when he was mourning his father's death. He told me, "If only someone would have listened to how much I was hurting, I don't think I'd be here right now." He was very clear and articulate about the fact that no one noticed why he was behaving badly, or that the change in his character coincided with his father's death. His sudden shift into acting out should have been a red flag to someone. Whether it was his mother, a teacher, or a social worker, someone should have seen his bad behavior for what it was: a sign that he was in pain and needed help to work through it. Instead they just saw him as a "bad kid," and they treated him like one.

Not having a Dad was a much too common trait with these young men. When I interviewed Lee he was 18 years old and just six weeks into serving a life sentence. He was known as a hit man for his gang. When I asked him about being given such a severe sentence, he told me he was seen as an habitual offender, such that after multiple brushes with the law he was done, no more second chances. Lee did have a father. He told me that his parents had visited him just a week ago for the first time. When his parents were leaving, his father had hugged him and said he loved him. Lee was then quiet for a few seconds, looked me in the eyes and asked me, "Why did he never do that before?" You could feel the lost love, the lost moments a father could have had with his son. I told Lee, "I don't know why." He walked out of the room a broken soul, and I felt broken for him.

I was left with that "I don't know." I was haunted by it. I wanted to have an answer and I felt inadequate for not having one. I don't know why fathers stop hugging their children or stop saying I love you. I could have tried to conjecture, played the part of the all-knowing psychologist and given him an explanation for his relationship with his dad, but it would have been cheap. The truth is that there are probably many reasons, but I didn't know them and besides, no Freudian theory was going to get him out of prison.

There was one guy that I only knew by his street name, Dirty Red. I never did hear his real name. He was a wild man...very charismatic, well spoken, polite, and one of the best conmen I'd ever met. This guy could have you handing him the keys to his cell if you let down your guard for more then five seconds. He had been a drug dealer, a hustler, a stick-up guy, anything to make a buck. He just got caught too many times. He was now serving 20-30 years. DR, as I called him by the end of our time together, had a theory about life that he wanted me to share with kids who were still in school.

He said, "Some people have an "A" life, with an A car, an A house, and an A wife, but some people don't...like me. Look at me, I'm living here in prison; this is a "D" life. But you know what? If you stay in school and can get a D, maybe you can get a C, and if you can do C work than maybe you can do B work, and if you can get a B then you can probably get an A, and then you can have that "A" life."

I asked Dirty Red, "If you know all this, why didn't you do it?"

He said, "I guess I knew it all, but I didn't have anyone in my life to help me. It's hard to believe in yourself when you live on the streets."

He was very interested in my work with schools. He saw me as a channel directly to kids and their parents. He knew what he wished he had been told as a young man, and saw me as his opportunity to give this important message to children who needed to hear it. His advice to all kids was to stay in school. If you're not in school then you're probably doing something illegal. He also told me to tell the parents I spoke with to take care of their children, because if they don't the gangs will. He said, "We will feed them, clothe them and give them gifts, and they will be ours." I think there's a passage in the Bible that's quite similar.....

I got to know most of these men by name, but prisoners are most commonly identified by their street name or prison number. They all have a number.

Prisoner 34876 was a pro at reading people. His criminal life finally ended after he decided to go big or go home. He told me it all started with stealing small stuff, maybe a CD, a cell phone, or a car radio, but he discovered it was too much work for the return. He was very business-minded. He had figured out on his own what the business world calls "leveraging your time." For prisoner 34876, making the most of his time meant stealing from big box stores like Walmart, Kmart, and Costco. He would walk into the back room, emitting an air of confidence, always acting like he belonged there. He would grab a big flatbed push cart, go out on the floor and load it up with high-end stuff...TVs, VCRs, computers, and then he would push the cart right out the front door, load his van, drive to a town an hour away, and sell it all. Then he'd hit the store in the next town and do it all again. On a good day he'd make a few thousand dollars.

When I asked how he avoided getting caught by undercover cops and store security, he told me he would case the store for them just like the security guys cased for bad guys. After some time of study he could tell the difference between who was security and who was a legitimate shopper by reading their eyes, body language, and the way they moved about the store. He told me that real shoppers have a more deliberate movement about them. He said if he got the wrong look or had a bad feeling about someone he'd walk out, hit a different store, and maybe come back a week later. One time he had loaded the push cart full of goods and made it as far as the exit doors when he got a bad vibe about a guy looking at him. He stopped in between the two doors at the exit and just before security hit him he grabbed the pay phone and started dialing. When the security guys asked him if he had paid for the items on his cart he told them he was talking to his grandfather, telling him what variety of tech stuff they had. He outsmarted them. Technically he never left the store, so there was nothing they could do. They told him to bring the stuff back in the store and next time to write it down on paper. He walked out that time, but he wasn't so lucky when he was busted with twenty thousand dollars worth of goods in the back of his van and no sales receipt.

This inmate was fascinated with business and finance, working with people, and working with money. I told him he would make a great stockbroker but 34876 didn't know what I was talking about. He'd never heard of such an occupation. I explained what a stock broker does and how they make money. He was stunned. He asked me "Is that legal?" I assured him that yes, its legal, and you can make good money, especially with the skill set he had. When we were done with the interview he thanked me for everything and said he was going to start on his brokerage license while in the big house. Who knows, your broker could have a more colorful past than you may know.

~

When you're on the inside and meet some of these guys, it's more than sad. It feels like a waste of humanity, a waste of potential, not to mention how much money we waste to keep them locked up.

As of 2009 the United States has incarcerated almost 2.3 million men and women. Our prisons and jails cost us 52 billion dollars annually. In the state of Michigan we currently have approximately 44,000 inmates in prison and the annual budget for the Michigan Department of Corrections is 2.2 billion dollars.

The prisoners I met knew what they did was wrong, and at some point during our chat I would always ask, "Why did you do it?" The answer that kept coming back to haunt me was: "I didn't care," or "I don't care." After hearing this time and time again it finally occurred to me to ask, "When did you stop caring?" The answer was simple and straightforward: "When I stopped being cared for." Oh, that makes sense. Not being cared for came at a very early age for most of these guys.

During an interview one day I noticed a fluttering sound behind me, and turned to see that a butterfly had flown through the bars of the small, lone window of our interview room and was trapped inside. I tried to ignore the sound of its wings beating against the wall, but eventually I excused myself from the conversation and made it my mission to get this butterfly back outdoors. As I stood on a chair and attempted to use my notebook to coax the creature towards the open air, Joey, the young inmate I was speaking with, cheered me on from the table below. At first, every time I would get the butterfly near the window it would flit back towards the ceiling. I was so frustrated that for a moment I thought about using my notebook to whack it against that wall instead, simply ending the whole struggle. For some reason though, that wasn't really an option. I think I sensed that there was already enough pain and loss in this room. It took a few tries, but eventually I got the butterfly to land on the bars of the window then in an instant it was gone, flying free once more. "Oh!" exclaimed Joey. "You got him out!" I turned to see a huge smile on his face. He was so happy that this little butterfly was no longer stuck behind prison walls. I was happy too, until it hit me: I couldn't do this for Joey. I couldn't correct whatever mistake had brought him here, and I couldn't bring him out with me when I left that day. I couldn't set him free.

I wanted to meet the statistics, but who I met were a lot of really good guys, good people, that just happened to have acted out some really bad behaviors. Most of them never had a first chance in life, much less a second or third. As I sat on the other side of the table from these young men and listened to them talk about themselves, at times it seemed to me that I was the first person who had ever asked them who they are, how they feel about what's happened to them, and why it happened. I still don't have the answers, but I can't help thinking that if someone had cared for them and listened to them sooner, they would still be a person with the name that was given to them at birth and not just a number.

Killer Stars

I remember the first time I realized that I could die from something completely out of my control. This idea struck me one night on what was going to be my first true overnight campout. I was about seven or eight years old. My camping partners were my older brother Kevin and my first cousin Brian, who was a city kid. We were going to sleep under the stars on a warm summer night in a field about a quarter of a mile south of our farm house. As kids, we referred to that area as "across the creek."

There was a two-track path created by the weaving of farm tractors moving from field to field. We followed this as our hiking trail from our backyard across a field to a small stone bridge that we would cross to get to yet another field.

The spot chosen for our camp-out was just across the creek on top of a small hill with a couple of large maples. To us it was an idyllic little piece of nature. On a hot summer day the shade of the trees and the sound of the creek running over the rocks making up our rustic bridge seemed like paradise. It wasn't too far from our house, but it was far enough to count as a real camping trip out in the wilderness and all on our own.

We laid out our sleeping bags, built a fire, and talked—I

have no idea what the topic of these deep conversations was, but considering we were all under the age of twelve, I'm sure it was important and deserved to be recorded for all time. Alas, these brilliant conversations are now lost forever. Too bad for the future of mankind.

As the fire burned down and sleep was upon us, I remember seeing a shooting star.

"Hey, you guys! Did you see that?"

"Yeah," they both said.

"Well, where's it going?"

"It'll hit the earth somewhere," they said.

"What!? Hit the earth? You mean a star could fall and hit one of us while we're sleeping?"

"Yes, and if it does, you're dead!"

I lay there quietly, thinking to myself, "Do I want to risk this? I don't want to die on my first camp-out." I kept thinking about what it would be like to get hit by a huge fireball rock, crashing into me as I laid there sleeping.

I got up and said, "No way! I'm going home."

They both sat up in their sleeping bags and said "What?"

My mind was made up. "I'm going home."

"You're not going to get hit by anything," they said.

"You don't know that. I'm not getting killed by a falling star!"

I got out of my sleeping bag and rolled it up angrily. Both my brother and Brian tried talking me out of leaving, but there was no way I was going to sleep under the stars and maybe be killed by one. As I started walking back home on the path, by the light of the stars that weren't going to kill me, I could hear my fellow campers yelling for me to come back. I ignored their pleas. Continuing back to our house in the dark, I was thinking to myself: "I'm not dying tonight. I've got bigger and better camp-outs to live for. If those guys get hit tonight, it's not my fault." After I crawled into the safety of my own bed, it occurred to me that maybe a burning star could come crashing through the roof of our house. I figured home builders must have already planned for that, because I've never heard of people being killed in their beds by falling stars. That night I prayed that my brother and cousin would be safe. I hoped to see them tomorrow. But this time, I was sleeping safely in my bed to see another day.

What strikes me most about this memory is my sheer, unbreakable conviction that my fear was valid. Despite my comrades' insistence that there was nothing to be afraid of, I stuck to my guns and trusted my gut.

In fact, not only did I trust my instincts, but I examined them and reasoned through the issue as well. Irrational as the notion may seem now, at the time it made perfect sense that something hot, falling from the sky at high speeds, had to touch down somewhere, and that somewhere could be right on top of my head. I knew houses to be strong, safe structures that guarded people against things that fell from the sky, like snow and rain, so why shouldn't my house be able to protect me from a displaced piece of molten rock from outer space? I felt that I was afraid for good reason, and I took steps to help myself out of this seemingly dangerous situation.

All children have irrational fears of monsters, ghosts and frightening intruders. It seems like children don't usually question their feelings in these situations, they just find something that makes them feel safe; a blanket, a night light, whatever they need to feel protected.

When we get older we still have fears, and just like the imagined fears of children, they are things that are out of our control. We worry about money, physical dangers like car crashes, and military threats from other nations. We don't see these fears as being irrational like we do the supernatural worries of children. As adults we can't duck out of the camp-out, so to speak. We have to face the "What ifs." We can't stay tucked away in our houses because we're afraid of what could happen. If something is out of our control we have to accept that and go on with our lives.

That doesn't mean that our fears aren't real. No matter where it comes from, that feeling exists and therefore it's valid. It's how we deal with our fears and feelings that make the difference. Nelson Mandela once said, "Courage is not the absence of fear but the triumph over it."

Move

A re things just coincidence or are we all where we're supposed to be?

When I was a freshman in college I had a near-death experience which called to mind this question.

It was the summer of 1982. I was working at a federally funded program on Grand Valley State University's campus for the summer. I was part of a landscaping crew made up of both students and civilians, performing what they called "campus beautification." We were a group of twelve guys, ranging from age twenty-two to the mid-thirties. You had to meet a low income criterion in order to get a spot on the crew for this work opportunity, and we were a pretty mismatched group of rag-tag, wandering souls. One guy was an artsy photographer who seemed to be mostly interested in wandering around taking pictures of things. On the other end of the spectrum there was a Vietnam Vet named Scott and his roughneck friend Dave, who had this job as a way to basically avoid being homeless. We had convinced the crew chief to let us work four ten-hour days as opposed to the usual Monday through Friday 9-5, which was rare at the time. We were very forward thinking, or at least we were looking forward to the long weekends. It was hard at first, but having that coming break, Friday through Sunday off, was glorious!

Scott and Dave, who knew each other well, were always on the scam to slack off work. They worked harder at not working than work itself. One weekend they invited me over to play cards and have a drink at Scott's place just a few miles from where I lived near campus. Not having a car at the time, I rode my bike over to this little gathering.

My first mistake was accepting their invitation. Something about these guys seemed shady, and I should have followed my instincts, which up until that point had always told me to stay clear of them. Once I arrived, my next mistake was giving into Scott's desire to show off his gun collection, one of which was an old twenty-two caliber handgun that resembled a World War II, German Luger.

When Scott sat down across from me with the pistol I felt very uncomfortable because, where I grew up guns weren't brought to the table. Firearms weren't a form of entertainment, and they certainly were never pointed at someone. My uneasiness really spiked when he started talking about shooting "gooks" in Vietnam. That's when he swung the gun around and stopped when it was pointing right at me.

I stared into this small black hole at the end of the gun barrel for just a few seconds, my mind racing with only one thought on repeat: "Doesn't he know you're never supposed to point a gun at someone?!" It was one of the scariest, most alarming, and yet inquisitive moments of my life, staring into a small diameter black hole, just three feet away. I was electrified yet paralyzed, not knowing what to do. I sat in disbelief with that question running over and over in my head. "Doesn't he know you never point a gun at someone?!"

Now, this is the part of the story where things really start to get weird. All I can tell you is that this is the experience I had.

I sat frozen staring down the barrel of that gun until I heard a whisper, a voice in my left ear, demanding, yet calm and comforting at the same time. The voice said, "Move." That's it, just one word. One time. Nothing to be confused about. "Move."

So I did. I moved. I leapt to my right just as the gun went off. By the time I hit the floor, I knew I was hit. The other sensation that filled me was the concussion of sound. What I remember is how loud it was. The sound of the gun's explosion was almost palpable, and it reverberated through the room, ringing in the air long after the gun had been shot. I noticed a lot of pain coming from my left bicep and a sensation of wetness. I looked at my arm. Blood was running down it.

To add to the confusion, before I even had time to understand or process how badly I was hurt, I heard the girlfriend of the guy who just shot me yelling, "It's the second time you've done that!" She kept saying that one phrase over and over. I'm thinking, "I'm the second guy he's done this to? Did the other guy come out of this alive?" Not only was he not taking action to help me, but on top of everything I had to wonder if he was going to finish the job and kill me right then and there. Eventually, his girlfriend ran out of the house, which was a relief from her yelling that phrase over and over. She ran out and never came back.

I stood up, and with my right hand I felt my face to make sure it was still there. I ran to the bathroom and looked in the mirror. I had little specks of blood all over my face. I looked down at my arm, and with the blood flowing from it I couldn't tell if it was a big cut or if the bullet had gone straight through. I grabbed a towel, wrapped it around the source of the blood, and twisted it tightly with my right hand. I splashed cold water on my face, trying to wash off the smattering of blood and snap myself back to reality.

Eventually Scott and Dave showed up at the door of the bathroom, and I told them, "Don't say a word." I couldn't stand to hear them say, "I'm sorry." Any version of an apology couldn't possibly make up for what had just happened. All I knew was that I wanted to get out of there. Dave, who had witnessed everything, put my bike in the trunk of his car and gave me a ride home. I consoled myself with the thought that at least it was just my bike being stuffed into the trunk and not my dead body.

As we drove back, Dave asked me what I was going to do. I said, "Well, I think this cut needs stitches. Maybe I'll go to a med center." Dave replied, "You can't do that. If they find out what really happened, Scott might not miss next time." It was a transparently veiled threat that I was to keep my mouth shut about the entire incident if I knew what was good for me. The message was short but clear. Obviously Scott had no qualms about shooting a gun, and I knew what he was capable of.

That night I put tape around my arm, holding it tightly closed, figuring I'd get something more permanent tomorrow. The shock of what had happened kept slowly creeping into my body, shutting down the pain receptors. It was like I had taken a painkiller that was increasing in intensity and then wearing off intermittently, bringing the pain flooding back.

I fell asleep that night with images of the incident playing over and over again in my head. I would start to doze off and then suddenly the whole scene would come back to me...the sound of the gun exploding, the pain in my arm and seeing my blood flowing out of the wound. I eventually fell asleep, knowing that I had almost died. I could have been killed. I had come so close; too close. The shock put me in a strange emotional state of controlled rage. The images of the shooting visited me in and out of sleep. The question that kept coming back was, "What if I hadn't moved?" That voice I heard, warning me of danger, was a secret that I would keep for many years. It was too strange and inexplicable for me to even fully accept it, much less to attempt to explain the experience to other people.

I awoke the next morning feeling like I had been hit by a truck. Only my left arm had been hit, but for some reason the entire left side of my body ached from head to toe. The shock had lifted, leaving behind it an intense pain and the realization that my body had gone through a major trauma. I slowly got out of bed and looked out my bedroom window. Suddenly I saw the world in a different light. The greens of the grass and leaves seemed more vibrant than I'd ever remembered seeing before. The sounds of birds heightened as everything seemed more vivid, clearer, and more intense. I saw the outside world humming with life and realized that I was alive too. I get to see this again. I get to experience life. I survived.

I remembered reading of and hearing about a transformation in people who had encountered a near death experience...a kind of awakening. I thought, "I'm in it. This is happening to me." The feeling was so overwhelming that I knew it wouldn't last. It couldn't. It was too intense an emotional state to live like this forever.

I felt a strong longing to go see people. I felt like Ebenezer Scrooge at the end of *A Christmas Carol*. I wanted to run through the streets and hug everyone I saw and celebrate being alive. At the time I lived on a gravel road in the country, so the only living beings I would be able to hug would be cows and sheep. I don't even think I ate breakfast; I just got dressed and left the house. I rode my bike to the nearest commercial building, which was a bank, thinking I'd see people there, but it was closed, still too early in the morning. I thought, "I'll ride another mile to campus. Someone must be there by now."

When I reached campus I found myself getting off my bike and walking down the sidewalk. Subconsciously I must have known that if I was riding my bike, I wouldn't be able to talk with anyone. As I got into the heart of campus, I came across an older gentleman dressed in a maintenance uniform, pushing a big gray plastic barrel on a set of wheels, full of mops and brooms. We came together and stopped for a moment, looking at one another. He then took a survey of the clear blue sky, looked back at me and said, "It's a beautiful day." I thought to myself, "Buddy, you have no idea how beautiful this day is!" We fell easily into conversation, chatting about this day, my life as a student, his life as a maintenance man. We reached the point when a conversation with a stranger would usually end, and I thought he was going to shake my hand and say, "It was nice to meet you." Instead he asked if he could share some parting ideas with me. "Sure," I said. He must have sensed that I would be open to listening to what he had to say. When I think back on it, an old philosophical saying comes to mind, one that I've always found to be true: "When the student is ready, the teacher will appear."

The man began by saying, "Don't complain about Mondays." How did he know that I did?

He continued, "People complain about going to work on Mondays...and when do they start complaining? They start complaining on Sunday night. When you add it up that's fifty-two Mondays per year, plus Sunday nights. That's a lot of time to be miserable. Instead of complaining you should be glad you're alive to enjoy that Monday." I was speechless, except to stutter, "Yes."

Then he added, "Don't listen to the weather man. You know

how in the morning if you're watching TV or listening to the radio, the weatherman will say things like, 'It's nasty out there, it's miserable, it's gloomy?' Well, it's not. It's just the weather. You decide what kind of day it's going to be. Don't let someone else label the day or dictate what kind of day it's going to be. That's for you to decide. Besides, it's never the weather; it's what you're wearing."

Yeah, he's right. How many times have I heard the meteorologist use those exact words? Who do they think they are to tell me what kind of day it's going to be?

His final thought to me was, "Don't talk about what you're going to do. Just do it. It's much more impressive."

He's right, again. So many times I've tried to impress someone by talking about what I was going to do, and then never even came close to starting it!

At that, we shook hands and parted ways. He had no idea how deeply he impacted my life, or did he? Maybe he saw my open soul and took the opportunity to plant a few seeds of wisdom.

~

Eight years later I was working on campus teaching students with learning disabilities. Through the classroom doorway I saw this same man walk past my door, pushing that same gray barrel full of mops and brooms. It's him. It's William, the maintenance man. I remember seeing that iron-on name patch on his breast pocket. I told the kids to write their names a thousand times and that I'd be right back. They all looked at me with a face of, "Do what?" I didn't care. I just needed to reconnect with this man who had intervened at a critical moment in my life.

I walked out of the room, and by the time I reached him he

had set up the yellow plastic tent that says, "Bathroom Closed." I yelled, "William!" It took a few seconds, but he emerged through the doorway wearing yellow rubber gloves. I put my hand out to shake his, and he said, "My hands are dirty."

"I don't care," I said. "Do you remember me?"

He looked me over and nodded, "Yes."

I said, "William, years ago you told me three things that I have never forgotten. As a matter of fact, I've told others of your wisdom. I can't remember much of what was said in all those hours of college lectures from Ph.D.s, but I will never forget what you told me."

William started to tear up. A tear fell from his eye and rolled down his face. I said, "What's wrong, William?"

He choked back his cry and said, "You have no idea how much that means to me right now in my life."

"Well, it's true." I said. "I will always be grateful for the lessons you taught me."

The day I needed to hear his words, he was there for me. The day he needed to hear my words, I was there for him. Was it coincidence or are we all where we're supposed to be?

How do you stay in touch with the simple joys in life, keeping your mind and heart open to the lessons that can be learned in everyday experiences? Do you pray, thanking God for the things you have? Do you meditate, focusing on your breath and how grateful you are just to have that breath, to be alive? Is it hugging someone every day and reminding each other that you have someone who loves you?

Whatever it is, I believe it's important to find ways to remind ourselves every day that life is precious. We don't need to wait for fate to step in or for a catastrophe to happen to remind us that it could all be taken away.

After note:

In this experience, I followed my instincts many times. The voice that I heard telling me to move out of that chair was a type of instruction. I trusted that voice and followed the order. My overwhelming desire to be with people after the incident was also an instinct I followed, which led me to William. His instincts must have told him that I was open to hearing what he had to tell me that day. When I saw him years later I could have let him pass by, but I trusted my urge to speak with him, to let him know how much my encounter with him had touched me. This allowed me to return the favor, telling him something he needed to hear.

On that day after the shooting, I was awake, alive and ready to receive William's simple words of wisdom. I think that if we can try to be as open as I was that day after I cheated death; if we can be aware of the prompting of our intuition and listen to it, we might find opportunities to connect with others in ways that will change lives.

Beginner's Mind: Act II

SCARY FAIRY

This play recounts events as they truly occurred.
(Malcolm is about three years old. He prematurely lost his first tooth in a somewhat traumatic manner during an accident that occurred while jumping on the bed with his older sister. Long story short, his tooth ended up in the top of her skull. His parents, Anne and Tim, sit down that evening before bed to talk to Malcolm about the Tooth Fairy money exchange).

TIM AND ANNE
(enter Malcolm's bedroom with tooth wrapped in toilet paper)
Malcolm, we're going to put your tooth under your pillow so the Tooth Fairy can get it tonight.

MALCOLM
Who's the Tooth Fairy?

TIM AND ANNE

Well, she is a fairy that collects teeth from little kids after they've lost a tooth. She'll take the tooth and leave money under your pillow.

MALCOLM

How does she get into the house?

TIM AND ANNE

She comes in either through the window or the door.

MALCOLM

What's she going to do when she's in here? What door is she going to come in? Are the doors and windows going to be locked?

TIM AND ANNE

She's just going to take your tooth and leave you money.

MALCOLM

I don't want her coming in my room.

TIM AND ANNE

But she's going to give you money.

MALCOLM

What is she going to do with my tooth?
(By this time Tim and Anne are totally stunned and stumped by this unexpected barrage of questions. It's obvious that Malcolm wants nothing to do with this midnight intruder.).

TIM AND ANNE

(Tim and Anne look at each other for what to do next)

Well, she makes things out of the little boys' and girls' teeth.

MALCOLM

I don't want her in here.

TIM AND ANNE

Well, what if we put it in Dad's office, and she can come get it in there?

MALCOLM

No. I don't want her to take my tooth.

TIM AND ANNE

We'll just keep it in the office then.

MALCOLM

I want Penguino in there to guard my tooth so she can't get it. (Penguino is Malcolm's small, stuffed animal penguin. Apparently, of all his stuffed animals he deemed Penguino the most intimidating and therefore the most suited to be the security guard).

TIM AND ANNE

Ok. We'll set Penguino next to your tooth on Dad's desk.

(The next morning Malcolm wakes and checks on his tooth. It's still there, and would stay forever in a little blue box in his parents' possession).

Thoughts on "Scary Fairy"

Malcolm was scared of this strange fairy, but he wasn't afraid to confront the unknown with honest curiosity.

Coming from an adult perspective, this seemed like easy money, but Malcolm didn't care about the money; he wanted to feel safe in his bedroom.

If something seems strange, or you sense it's not quite right and you don't trust it, the beginner's mind wants to stop, question it, listen to it. Don't ignore those thoughts and feelings just because it's the status quo.

The beginner's mind might need support, back-up. Trust your gut on choosing an ally, a protector of what is irreplaceable to you. Even if that defender is six inches tall, doesn't make a sound, and cannot move.

Find your own Penguino who will never leave your side.

Thank you Malcolm for reminding me to trust my gut, to ask "Why?" and to defend what's priceless.

THE END

Saying Yes

I 'm not sure how he found me, and I can't remember under what circumstances I agreed to the job, but I said 'yes' to a world out of my league. The 'yes' was working with a high-tech company that made a device called a densitometer, among other high-tech equipment.

Basically, these devices analyzed color for the printing industry. Whatever shade of color you desired, this densitometer could read it and tell you exactly what pigments of colors you needed to mix together to get the original color—not close, but precisely the original color. This high-tech company sold their equipment around the world but was headquartered in Grand Rapids, Michigan.

Ian, my contact from the company, and the guy I had said 'yes' to, was a brilliant, fast-talking, marketing/PR person. He knew this equipment like the engineers who built it. I, on the other hand, had never felt so overwhelmed and inadequate in a job before. Ian would rattle off information about the densitometer, and I remember nodding my head pretending I understood what he was talking about. In reality I was thinking, "How much am I being paid for this job?"

The job I had said 'yes' to was to get on stage at industry trade shows, educating and entertaining whomever filled the seats at our elaborate display booth. This very expensive, custom built, show place to display the densitometer was going to be a first for this company. Part of the space they would be renting at these upcoming tech conventions was seating. I was hired to come up with some type of fun, engaging, interactive show that would draw in the wandering, bag carrying, zombie-like people, attending the convention. I had to lure them away from all the other businesses vying for their attention. The more space you rent, the more you spend. Therefore whatever show I created had better be good, because a lot of money was being invested.

I'd never done anything like this or attended anything like this, other than an auto show. So, I was really creating a program for an audience I didn't know or understand, in a venue I didn't understand. I visualized myself as a barker on the midway at the fair calling out, "A quarter to play, a quarter to win, come on in!" That was the phrase I was taught to say when I was fourteen working the ring toss game at the Ionia Free Fair. I'd said 'yes' to this job, too. I worked kiddie rides and hotdog sales as well, always focused on drawing people in to spend money. This was back in the day when they still had freak shows, and a guy would stand outside, calling for people to come witness the oddities, the two-headed calf, snake lady, and pop-eye, who could pop his eyeballs out of their sockets on demand.

Looking back at that summer job, I realized I was in over my head then too, especially working the hot dog trailer. I had never made change before, and I was really bad at math. I remember selling x number of hotdogs to someone and just guessing how much to give them in return. I was angrily accused of ripping people off, and at other times people looked at me like, "Are you paying me to eat here?"

One time a couple of rough looking, black leather vest wearing, motorcycle gang guys wanted a deal on hot dogs. They knew they could intimidate me. They asked for half off. Once I did that deal, they told me a lot more of the gang was coming, and they wanted the hot dogs for free or they'd hurt me. They walked away. The other kid I was working the trailer with asked, "What are you going to do?" I told him, "Start getting a bunch of hot-dogs ready because when these guys come back it's going to be free dog night. I'm not dying because I held out on a hotdog."

So here I was again, working a job I'd never done before, improvising, creating and figuring out some way to make it work. I was getting really worried about how I was going to pull this off.

The new display was being built in Chicago, dates for trade shows were being organized, and here I sat in my little office at home thinking, "What can I do?" Then my eye suddenly caught the sight of the spine of a book on my shelf that read: *The Lüscher Color Test: The Remarkable Test that Reveals Your Personality Through Color.* That's all I needed to know—whatever this book was, I was somehow going to make it work. I flipped the book over and on the back cover was a warning that read: IMPORTANT— This book is intended to be used and administered by licensed psychiatrists, psychologists, and physicians only. I thought to myself, "Perfect! This is exactly what I need."

Here's the deal, this Dr. Max Lüscher was born in Basel, Switzerland in 1923. He became a well known psychologist throughout Europe. He developed and administered his color test on both individuals and corporations. For example, he chose all the colors for all the Volkswagen plants in West Germany. In the center of the paperback version are two pages of punch-out color cards. You remove the cards at the perforated edge and wind up with eight different colored cards. You're ready to start testing—if you're a licensed professional, that is...which I suddenly became.

As a newly minted psychological professional, I would administer the test by asking my "patient" to pick their favorite colors out of the eight cards and place them in order of preference. Each card had a number on the back. So, let's say you laid out your favorite color cards in a combination of yellow, red, green, blue. I would flip the cards over to find the numbers on the back, in this case they would be: 4, 3, 2, 1.

I would then turn to the interpretation tables of the book, which according to the sequence of numbers would offer a description of your personality. In this example the analysis would read "Active, outgoing, and restless. Feels frustrated by the slowness with which events develop." This is what I was preparing to do at the convention. I would analyze people in front of other people at the trade show based on their colors, and find a way to work in how great our densitometers were at analyzing color too.

When I told the convention committee my plan, they all looked at me with blank expressions.

Someone said, "You're joking, right?"

"No." I said. "It will be great. It's interactive, it deals with colors, and it will be funny, too."

"How is this going to be funny?" Another person asked.

"Well, I will read a person's profile and then make fun of how psychologically disturbed they are."

One out of about fifteen people at this meeting laughed and agreed it would be funny.

The next thing I know, I'm on stage at the San Francisco Conference Center, luring suspicious conference attendees into my booth to enjoy the amazing color analysis where I can read people's personalities just by the way they arrange their favorite colors.

People were eager to witness, but slow to volunteer. Everyone loved the idea of seeing this done, but we had planned on some reluctance from volunteers, so I bribed the audience with special gifts...umbrellas, hats, t-shirts, but only if they volunteered to be part of the show. It's amazing what people will do for a t-shirt. With a hand-held mic, I was able to make comments while my 'victim', I mean my willing conference attendee, arranged their colors. I'd say things like, "Oh, I see you have a lot going on in your life right now," or "Wow, I want to party with you some-time!" The audience response varied depending on what I said about a volunteer's personal issues during the color analysis.

I tried to keep the color analysis game show lighthearted, but I did have a few people ask me to do a little more analysis which I found clever ways of avoiding. I discovered that if people thought I had a little insight into their psyches, they wanted more answers to their troubles. That was the first and last time I a worked high-tech trade show or attempted to do therapy using Lüscher's color test.

Those days of performing the color analysis game show felt like weeks. I didn't have any soulful connection to the product. It held no meaning for me. I said 'yes' to this job, ended up being in way over my head, dug myself out, and found a way to make it work. However, I realized through this experience that I hated working trade shows. At a certain point it didn't matter how much I was being paid, the answer, I discovered to trade show work, is just 'no.'

It's an interesting dilemma when you find yourself at the crossroads to saying 'yes' or 'no' to a job opportunity. I have expe-rienced both triumph and failure after answering 'yes' to a job proposal. As a performer I've learned, I can't mold myself into doing just anything. It has to feel authentic. And, you don't know unless you try.

When you carry within you, like I do, the entrepreneurial DNA that's been passed down from 'make or break' Irish roots, navigating your work life isn't a perfect science; never has been, never will be. You go with your gut. You do the best you can and learn to live with the outcome. When you fail it hurts, its embarrassing, it never really leaves you, but the only way to know is to try. Hikers use stacks of stones called cairns (e.g. book cover) to act as landmarks, letting others know that they're headed in the right direction, that they're on the right path. My job failures act as cairns, alerting me to the wrong path and pushing me in the right direction in my future work and life travels. This is the reason that when the phone rings, asking me to do a job, to try something new, I push myself to keep saying 'yes.'

V.
HONEST
EMOTIONS

As Low as Dirt

The Latin root for humiliation—humus—means earth, the ground. You've hit dirt. You can't get any lower. Why does humiliation feel so bad? How can it be so overwhelmingly painful? One area in life that we experience humiliation the most is when we are trying to learn something new. Often we fail on the first try, and we feel angry, frustrated, and humiliated. I think it hurts so much because you know how to do so many other things without even putting too much effort into it. Now, here's this seemingly simple task that you can't seem to figure out. It's almost as if you've been given a test but you didn't get to study for it.

I'm terrible at reading instructions. As soon as I unfold that pamphlet with diagrams and numbers and words all mixed together, I'm immediately lost. It might as well be in Swahili. In fact, the French and Spanish translations included in the manual make me feel even more stupid, reminding me that I can't speak any foreign languages. I remember getting so ticked off putting together my first grill with the help of my wife. Instead of laughing about how these directions were written by a bunch of zoo animals, I got crazy mad. It was one of those rites of passage for a young couple. It was our first try as husband and wife at assembling something for our first home. It should have been a fond memory, but instead of having fun and laughing at my inability to follow directions, I got mad. That's the memory I gave myself.

Since then I've made some pretty radical changes in my attitude. I tell myself, no more getting mad. Swearing? Sometimes. Anger? No.

I recently bought a ping-pong table that came in a huge box, so big and heavy that it wouldn't fit through our back door. My son and I opened it outside and carried it to the basement in pieces. Per usual, the guy at the sporting goods store had said, "Oh, yeah, it's super easy to set up. Just takes a few minutes!" Two hours later, my son Malcolm, my wife Anne, and I stood proudly staring at our new ping-pong table. It was not easy to do. If I had been left on my own to do this, that table would still be lying in parts on the floor of our basement. This time I never got angry, not even frustrated.

My son is really the reason why I didn't go there. He's good at putting things together by using written directions and pictorial diagrams—maybe because he's assembled more pieces of Lego parts than there are stars in the universe. For the most part he's able to keep his cool. He's just learned somehow to take it on more as a challenge, another puzzle, than as an assault on his intelligence. Instead of a Lego Star Wars fighter jet, it's just a ping-pong table.

⌒

At age 13, Malcolm joined the seventh grade basketball team. The team requires all its members to wear a tie on game days, and today is a game day, a tie day. Until today, I've tied the tie for him the night before. However, last night he wanted to learn how to do it himself. As he was practicing I heard him say, "I'm not good at doing things like this. I can't do this." In other words, "This is humiliating. I've hit dirt. I'm as low as I can go." It hurt to hear that, because I know I've said that same thing out loud for him to hear. I don't want him thinking that way, feeling that way.

The season ended with a somewhat mediocre record, but nonetheless there was a team banquet celebrating their accomplishments. Little did I know that at the banquet that night I would have to face my own fear of doing something new and possibly humiliating for both myself and my son.

The coach had asked all of the fathers to purchase a journal and write an entry to their sons. Totally unexpectedly that night, he asked each of us fathers to read aloud to the whole group what we had written. I wrote to my son with the idea that it would be for his eyes only. Had I known that my words would be on public display, I'm sure I would have written something different, probably something less personal. I reluctantly agreed to read it aloud, as did all the other dads.

At first thought my critic's voice said, "What you wrote isn't good enough. You're going to sound stupid." I have bad memories of being made fun of in school for stumbling over my words when reading out loud in class. I could humiliate both myself and my son by reading aloud what I wrote and getting emotional in front of everyone. The more I thought about it, though, the more I concluded that it can't be wrong or stupid, because what I wrote to my son was honest, true, and out of love.

To lighten the mood before reading the personal words that were meant for my son, I got up in front of the group, holding up the cheap $1.50 Walgreen's notebook that I had purchased for the occasion. Many of the fathers had bought leather-bound journals.

As I held mine up I said, "As you can see I spent a lot of money on my son's journal." This got a bit of a laugh, and I continued by ad-libbing the fictitious first line of the journal entry. I opened with, "Dear son, I am, and will always be, a superior athlete. You will never come close to my athletic abilities." People slowly started to realize that this was a joke and began to laugh. Then I cut the crap and read aloud what I had written:

To my son Malcolm,

Do you remember the time I asked you, "Do you believe God loves your heart?" and you said, "Yes."

I also asked you, "Do you love God?" and you said, "Yes."

I believe you have a wonderful, big, loving heart, and you will make a great difference in the world by staying true to your heart. I love you more than you will ever know.

YOUR DAD!

By the time I finished, Malcolm had been moved to tears, as were many of the moms in the audience. The other fathers held their emotions at bay while reading their journal entries, but it wasn't easy. All of them struggled not to cry, not to be humiliated by tears.

This experience helped to remind me that we should never be ashamed of sharing our feelings with someone we love. That doesn't mean that it's always easy to voice our emotions to some-one else. It can be very scary to "put ourselves out there," because we risk humiliation, but taking that risk is what makes sharing our feelings with others such a special experience.

If we get frustrated when learning something new, we can stop, address our anger, and call it what it really is: humiliation. When we inevitably fail to do this novel task perfectly on the first or second try, we often say things like, "I'm just not good at this type of thing," or especially when we're young we say, "I don't care." Really, we do care. We care so much that we're upset over not being able to do it. This is when we can try to remind ourselves that there's no reason to be ashamed. We just don't know how to do this thing yet, whatever that thing may be. It's also a great opportunity to model this behavior for the next generation. It shows others that it's okay to falter and struggle with a new task, and it's also okay to express our feelings of vulnerability about it.

When we feel ashamed, when we're as low as dirt, it's part of the human experience. If we pick ourselves up from the dirt, dust it off, and keep trying, in that simple act, we have triumphed.

Coming Home

It was just another commuter flight filled with a bunch of people just like me, trying to get to our destinations safe and on time. The back of my seat was in its upright position, tray table locked in place, seat belt secured, and I did it all by myself, without the aid of the flight attendant. All electronic devices had been turned off. We were pushing back from our gate when a flight attendant came over the intercom and in an atypically cheery voice said, "Hey everyone! We have on board with us a returning soldier from Iraq. It's his first time home in over a year."

The crowded plane erupted in applause while we all started looking around to see who it was. What did he look like? Was he okay? He reluctantly identified himself. Sitting in the very back seat, dressed in civilian clothes, he waved with a shy look of gratitude. You could tell he didn't ask for this recognition and he was pretty uncomfortable with it.

I was sitting just a few rows ahead of him. I turned around and found his eyes darting frantically. I stayed focused on him until our eyes locked. I smiled and gave him a thumbs-up sign. He nodded back with a smile of recognition.

The flight attendant had started our beverage service when I stopped her and asked about buying our soldier a beer. She said, "He's already getting what he wants." "Right on!" I thought. "He deserves a little pampering." You could feel an unspoken bond developing throughout the plane during the unanimous applause for our returning solder. It's as if we were now a part of bringing him home. We had a mission. It felt good. We had all been brought together by one guy coming home. It felt much bigger than any one of us.

There are a few things that will act as conversation starters with a seatmate on a plane. A really loud crying baby will do it, so will heavy turbulence, but the most common conversation starter is the captain's voice announcing an unexpected delay. When the bad news is delivered the passengers let out a collective groan, a choir singing notes of disappointment. There's a lot of eye rolling, and those who were sitting up at attention to hear the message sink back in their seats with a deep sigh of frustration. Misery loves company, so we talk. But today we didn't turn to the person seated next to us to ask, "What do you do?" or to commiserate about the trials and tribulations of air travel. The topic of everyone's conversation was this soldier, our fellow passenger, coming home from war.

Eventually we arrived safely at our destination. During our taxiing toward the gate, phones were turned on, people began gathering their goods, and yet there was a feeling in the air that we were all preoccupied with the knowledge that our soldier was home. Normally by the time a plane stops at the jet bridge, people are out of their seats, opening overhead compartments, and impatiently waiting for their turn to step into the aisle and exit the plane. This time was different. That same enthusiastic flight attendant's voice came back, and said, "If you don't mind, our returning soldier has some very anxious people waiting to see him. If you could remain seated so he could get off first it would be appreciated." Everyone froze in their seats. As he walked from the back of the plane towards the front, I was filled with a sense of pride. I felt honored to be part of his safe homecoming. Once again the plane erupted in applause. He stopped at the front just before exiting, turned to face us, waved, and mouthed the words, "Thank you!" With that he was gone.

There was something profound about the moment after his exit. We remained seated for a couple of seconds, letting the magnitude of what we had just witnessed sink in, contemplating what it really means to come home.

How do you put into words the anticipation of seeing someone you love for the first time after a long separation? I think part of the suspense around waiting to see someone at the airport is in the not knowing, because until you see that person with your own eyes, hold them in your arms, it's not yet real. Often it's not until visual and physical contact have been made that our emotions really hit us. How many times have you exited a plane and seen passengers walking towards the person waiting for them. They seem fine, walking calmly, but when they catch sight of their loved ones, and hugs are exchanged, suddenly the tears start to flow.

We were so happy for the returning soldier because we also knew that coming home from war isn't always joyful.

The war in Iraq had been going on for about six years when I was seated on yet another plane and again witnessed a soldier coming home.

By the time we landed, it was dark. As we got closer to our gate, I noticed more people than usual on the tarmac and extra outdoor lighting around the plane outside my window. When we came to a stop, I saw what was happening.

Instead of the flight attendant letting us know that it was okay to get up, the captain came over the intercom. He said, "I would like everyone to hold fast for a couple of minutes while our military performs a ceremony that is taking place at the plane to our left side." I saw the large cargo door open. A number of soldiers appeared, rolling into place a metal gurney. A casket was being carefully carried out of the belly of the plane, placed on the gurney, and wheeled away. I could hear whispers of information being passed around, letting everyone know what we were seeing on our side of the plane. Everyone on board our full flight was suddenly very quiet, very sad. We all knew that there would be no joyful homecoming for this soldier. No hugs, no kisses...but there would probably be lots of crying.

Again I witnessed a plane full of strangers bonded by a single soldier coming home. Instead of leaving with applause as we had with the safely returned soldier, a somber mood washed over everyone on board, and we exited in relative silence.

If this story leaves you feeling sad and empty, that makes sense. In our society we are so far removed from war. We hear about the dead, but we never see them. We may come across an obituary in the paper with a picture of a smiling and hopeful young soldier, but we don't see the casket and the folded flag. I wish there was a happy ending or redeeming note, but it's simply a true story of what happened, what I saw that night.

I've shared both parts of this story with groups that I speak to. Everyone loves hearing the happy homecoming. However, the soldier coming home in a casket leaves people numb. They don't know what to say. They're emotionally caught off guard and really have no response to it. When I've encouraged people to give me some kind of feedback, to say *something*, the most common response I get is, "Well, I just feel sad." One time someone volunteered, "I guess there are two ways to come home." So why tell it? What good can possibly come from this sad story?

Feeling sad can sometimes feel really uncomfortable. It feels wrong, and we just want it to go away...but sad things happen.

So what do we do with that sadness?

We can become more sensitive or compassionate. We can learn to empathize with others. We can grow from it and maybe help someone in their time of sorrow. It's different for everyone. People will learn different things from their sadness. So when something heartbreaking happens again, you could try thinking, "What did I do the last time I was sad?" and ask yourself,

"Can I let myself be sad?" Yes, you can.

"Can I learn from it?" Yes.

"Can I share it?" Yes.

"Will it help?" Sometimes.

It's Stupid

Watching the typical mayhem that occurs throughout an afternoon in the office of a middle school made up of 900 students is a fascinating experience. These offices aren't that big, and yet they act as the triage center for treating all of the little wounds that occur on any given day, everything from bandaging cut knees and calming stomach aches to acting as a therapy center for resolving disciplinary problems. On top of it all, the secretary is bustling around the office organizing activities for the entire school and running interference for the principal. The phone is constantly ringing, and the secretary is juggling it all while still asking me if I'd like a cup of coffee.

One day before giving an assembly, I sat motionless on a chair watching all of this unfold when a teacher arrived, pushed two teen boys through the doorway saying as she did so, "These two are not coming to the assembly." As she walked away with the remaining ten or so students, I knew then what was going on. Most classes in a school of this size have a minimum of 25 to 30 students, so I knew that this small class was different. These two boys were part of a Resource Room, also known as Special Ed.

The principal said, "Go into my office and wait. I'll be there in a few minutes." By the look of the boys and the worn out look of the teacher, I suspected that their choice to act out at this particular time had something to do with attending the assembly.

I asked the principal, "Hey do you mind if I have a talk with these two boys?"

"Help yourself," he replied.

I opened his office door. One of the boys was sitting in the principal's chair with his feet up on the desk. The other kid was looking through the knick-knacks on the shelf. When they saw me come in they both stood at attention, like it was military school, and acted like they were the most innocent children in the world.

I said, "What's going on?" Both looked at the floor and said, "Nothing."

"Oh, really? Why are you guys in here? The assembly is going to start soon."

"Our teacher said we can't go because we got in trouble."

"Oh, really? Well, don't you guys want to go to the assembly?" In unison they both replied with an emphatic, "No!"

"Why not?"

"Because it's stupid."

"What makes you think that? What's stupid about it?"

One of the boys said, "I don't know, it's just some stupid guy who's going to talk about something stupid."

I said, "Yeah, he's probably some stupid guy who thinks he knows it all, right?" They both looked at me, pleased with the fact that my idea was the same as theirs. I asked, "Do you know who the stupid guy is?"

They both said again, this time with a little more anger, "No, we don't."

I said, "Yes you do. It's me!" Their faces gave away their shock.

For a few seconds they didn't know what to say. Finally one asked, "Are we in big trouble now?"

"No, but let me guess what happened. You two don't want to be seen with the other Special Ed kids at the assembly, do you?"

They both paused then said, "The other kids will tease us when they see us coming into the assembly with our Resource Room class."

"So you deliberately got kicked out so you wouldn't be seen with your class at the assembly. Am I right?" They both seemed so relieved that I understood. I said, "I don't blame you. I hated being teased too."

"What were you teased about?" they asked. I told them that although I didn't have to go to a Resource Room, I did have to read out loud in front of the class, and I got teased because I couldn't read very well. They both seemed to know what I was talking about. I told them, "I'm going to be discussing this exact topic during the assembly." A big smile came to their faces. I could tell we were all on the same page now.

"So, do you want to come to the assembly and hear what I have to say?" Both boys appeared eager to hear about my story which seemed so similar to theirs. I told them to wait here, keep their feet off the principal's desk, and I'll work out a deal to get them back in on the action.

I told the principal what went down and that if anyone should be at this assembly it's these two boys. He agreed. Both boys sat with their Resource Room class. We exchanged knowing looks a few times throughout the assembly. We knew something that the others didn't.

When we're kids and we're afraid of something, as an excuse for avoiding it, we often say something like, "That's stupid." When things are hard for us as adults, "That's stupid" changes to "That's *really* stupid," or maybe something a bit more evasive like, "Well, I just don't like doing that kind of thing. It's boring." It's a mask that we wear, and that mask comes with a pretty bad attitude. Like those boys, the attitude doesn't line up with what's really going on inside.

Most of the time when people act out it's for a reason, and the reason won't always be directly related to their behavior. That's why you'll sometimes see a big fancy boat parked next to a little shabby house. You're supposed to be impressed, but when I see that I don't think, "Wow, that guy's got a big boat," I think, "Wow, that guy's got an even bigger problem."

Those boys weren't bad kids. They just didn't want to be embarrassed and teased. They didn't want to admit that they were hurting, so they said, "It's stupid." It's a coping mechanism to keep us safe from what we don't want to face, but that reaction will also keep us from hearing exactly what we really need to hear. As this story illustrates, the boys were willing to go to extreme measures to keep from being honest about their true feelings.

How many times have you said those words? "That's stupid." Really? Stupid? What did you really mean?

Just Ask

A s soon as I walked in I was struck by the sound of holiday
music being played on a piano, the notes filling the large
reception room. My first thought when I heard this beautiful
piano music was, "Wow! They must have hired a real professional
for this event." It was a holiday fundraising party at the Ronald
McDonald House, a program that offers housing to families who
need to live near a hospital while a family member seeks signifi-
cant medical treatment. After mingling for a while I ended up
standing around the hors d'oeuvres table where I casually asked
a man next to me how he was connected with the organization.
He said, "Well, tonight I'm the piano player." He was the man creating the lovely music I had heard when walking in. How could
this be? The man standing in front of me was balancing his plate
on the forearm of his right arm with a bunched up fist, leaning it
against his chest and eating with his left hand. It was obvious that
he had a physical impairment that left him with the use of only
one hand, and yet he played the piano. Our conversation immediately veered toward me asking how he was able to play the piano
with only one hand, and this is what I learned...

His name is Les. He was born with Cerebral Palsy (CP) and was raised in upstate New York. His grandmother told him at a young age that he had music inside of him, so he started playing piano with one finger, the index finger on his left hand, his good hand. His parents sent him to a private Christian school in Kentucky for four years of high school. He met a girl who lived in Michigan, and at age 29, with twenty dollars, he moved there, married that girl, had five children, and worked for Amway corporation for 32 years.

Les now volunteers for Ronald McDonald House as a driver. He chauffeurs people back and forth to the hospital, listening to them tell their stories of sick children, broken families, and hard times.

Hearing Les' story prompted me to want to share with him an experience I had with a high school boy who also had CP.

I was teaching a summer school theater class comprised of 8th through 12th graders. On the first morning we were all sitting in a circle on the floor of a large stage. While going around the circle introducing ourselves one last student showed up. The moment I saw him I knew there were issues to be dealt with. He stood about six feet tall and was slightly overweight. As he walked towards us, I noticed he carried his left arm up and close to his side, shuffled with a slight limp, and would periodically roll his head in a sweeping motion.

All eighteen of his soon-to-be fellow classmates watched silently as he walked into the theater. A few smirked. A few rolled their eyes. Some just looked at me with a look of, "What are we going to do with him?" One kid stuck out as being the consummate "cool guy." He had been wearing his sunglasses inside since we arrived. Everything about him oozed arrogance. I thought, "If anyone is going to cause trouble and resist participating in the activities, it's this kid." When the young man with the physical disability walked into the room I immediately thought, "This punk kid with the sunglasses is going to make fun of him and make life difficult for him."

When he made his way over to us I invited him to sit next to me on the floor. He said, "Can I sit in a chair? It's hard for me to get up off the floor." I said sure, and he pulled up a chair. Soon it was his turn to introduce himself. He simply said, "I'm going into tenth grade, and I'm from Sparta," which is a small rural town in Michigan. That's it. That's all he had to say about himself. I wanted to get him to say more, and I figured, why ignore the obvious?

I said, "I noticed when you walked into class that you have a slight limp, you hold your arm close to your side and it's hard for you to sit on the floor. Can you tell me about that?"

Suddenly the group got very quiet. "I have CP. It's Cerebral Palsy. I was born with it."

"Okay," I said. "Is there anything else we should know so we can keep everyone safe and have some fun?"

"Well, I can't run very fast." I assured him that it wouldn't be a problem. As I turned around to check in with everyone in the circle, I saw stunned faces...eyes wide open, mouths hanging, and just a look of, "I can't believe you just asked him what we were all thinking."

I knew I had to confront the prejudice, the awkwardness that people can have when they're around someone with a physical disability. After playing some of our initial theater games, most of which the boy with CP participated in with no problem, we took a break. The kid with the sunglasses, who I thought would give this boy the hardest time, took this opportunity to walk up to him. I overheard him asking in a cautious and curious manner, "Can you catch this CP stuff?" The young man just kind of laughed and said, "No, you can't get it from me. You're born with it." I was listening closely, ready to jump to the boy's defense if the talk turned mean. To my surprise the other boy answered, "Okay, I was just wondering," The two boys continued to have a normal high school guy conversation, consisting mostly of single syllable grunts. "Ugh." "Ugh." "Huh." If you don't believe in evolution just listen to a conversation between two teenage boys. It'll bring you right back to the cave.

At the end of the day I checked in with the boy and asked if he'd ever had another student ask him about his CP. He said, "No. Kids just laugh at me and make fun of me, but they never ask about it." It struck me as being so sad and so preventable. That day he wasn't made fun of, and all I had to do was ask.

I told this story to Les at the fundraiser, prompting him to tell me more about himself. Although he went on to marry, have children, and enjoy a long career and fruitful experience as a volunteer, growing up with CP was difficult. He was picked on by classmates, and no one ever asked him what was wrong; he just suffered silently. He was very touched by the story I told him. He said that he wished people would have asked him about his condition, that it would have helped him. To this day he wished that people would care enough to ask him what his life is like with cerebral palsy.

That night, playing beautiful music behind the grand piano, it was clear that he had carried with him his grandmother's statement that he had music inside him. His ability to play piano was a big part of what kept his sense of self-worth intact through all the hardship caused by his disability. That night he sat behind the piano, not to be seen but to be heard, playing with his good hand. I never would have known his story had I not just asked.

When we're young, and we wonder shamelessly why someone

is different, we're just being honest, naturally curious, and per-fectly innocent. Then we grow up, become smart, intelligent, sophisticated, and we stop asking.

Why is that? Because it's impolite? None of our business? Too invasive?

There's a guy I know, Reggie, with a medical condition called Neurofibromatosis (NF) where tumors can grow throughout the body causing major disfigurement. He was born with small tumors all over his body, and as he grew, the tumors grew with him. It was hard for Reggie to integrate just how much his body was morphing, because the change was so gradual. However, at the onset of puberty, the symptoms of his disease accelerated such that by the time he entered high school his face and body became so distorted that he started to hide. One day, while wait-ing for the bus after school a teacher walked past him, looked at him, and asked, "Where did you get that thing?" Confused, Reg-gie said, "What?" The teacher thought he was wearing a mask. Realizing his mistake he said, "Oh. Never mind," and walked away. No apology. No sign of remorse. It wasn't Reggie's first day of school. He was surprised that this teacher had never noticed him before; that the sight of his face seemed so inhuman that he assumed it was a mask, the face of a monster. This display hap-pened in front of all of his friends, and Reggie never forgot this humiliating moment.

This type of reaction to his disorder quickly became the norm. Everywhere Reggie went people stared at and mocked him. Eventually he began to turn his back on the outside world entirely. When his sister and brother went to the skating rink or the movies, Reggie stayed home. He would rather isolate himself than endure the pain and humiliation that the world offered him. Being constantly tormented by other kids and adults was just too painful. His family members stood up for him, but anyone who didn't know him ridiculed him.

Reggie's brother also suffered from NF and early in his life he passed away as the result of the disorder. This crushing blow made Reggie realize that he needed to do something; that he needed to raise awareness about NF. He reached out to Lou, a family friend, and asked him to make up a few t-shirts for him to wear around the neighborhood. The back of the shirt had an outline of his face, disproportionate and disfigured. On the front were printed two words: "Just Ask." He could tell that when he was out in public people wanted to know why he looked the way he did, but they didn't know that it was okay to ask. Just ask. That was his message to the world...and sure enough, people began to ask.

Lou encouraged Reggie to spread his message, and also to rejoin society. One day, Lou called and invited Reggie to a baseball game. Still plagued by his old fears, Reggie felt angry that his friend was asking him to engage in an activity that would cause him pain. There would be too many people, people that would make him feel humiliated. To make matters worse, Lou told him to wear the "Just Ask" t-shirt. This was only going to draw more unwanted attention! Despite all of this, Reggie fought against his feelings of dread and agreed to go for the sake of his friend. There was no way for him to know it, but wearing the shirt to the baseball game that day would change his life.

All of his fears turned out to be unfounded. Instead of stares, jeers, and people rudely asking, "What happened to you?" people began to ask in a different way. They were nice. This was a new experience for Reggie...strangers being nice to him. People asked to take pictures with him and expressed a genuine concern and interest in learning about NF. He suddenly felt like he had wasted years of his life hiding. People had been there all along, just waiting to accept him, and he never even gave them the chance.

Fueled by this positive experience, he felt encouraged to do more. He started going to more public events. The more places he went, the more people he met. These small steps to reenter the world snowballed into a lifestyle of educating people about the disorder that took his brother's life, and the many people like himself who lived with it every day. For the sake of people afflicted with NF, he wanted to be their spokesperson and share his story with those who knew nothing about the disorder. Soon he had a blog and a website. What was even more surprising to Reggie than all of this attention was that he started to make friends. For the first time in his life he was truly connecting with the world.

Reggie's message is that there is always hope, that life should be lived to the fullest. His other message of "Just Ask," has a caveat to it though. The people who still approach him at the airport or grocery store and ask with a hint of disgust, "What happened to your face?" simply aren't worth his time. It's pointless to try to explain himself to these people. He knows that anyone who would ask in such a mean way will never understand. In his words, he states that with these narrow-minded individuals, "I just leave them where they are." He knows that if these same people took the time to get to know him they would be shocked and offended to hear someone ask him about his appearance with such a malicious attitude. The many people who take the time to get to know him and become his friends would gladly go after anyone who mistreats him.

Reggie now gives public talks, telling his story and raising awareness about NF. He says, "A lot of times I don't know what I'm going to say. I don't have a speech writer. I just say what I feel, what I've experienced, and speak from my heart."

When I told Reggie about the boy whom I had asked to tell me about his CP, he pointed out two critical aspects of that situation. One was the way in which I asked and why. I asked out of genuine concern and care for his condition and how it affected his life. Again, Reggie's message is that it's not just asking, it's how you ask.

The second observation that he had is that by inquiring about the boy's condition I was modeling a behavior for the other kids who were present. What he liked so much about this is that the question brought that inner fear and discomfort out into the open. "You were right," he said. "They were all wondering the same thing you were." The problem was that they didn't know what to do with that thought, that question. They didn't know it was okay to just ask.

In your journey through life, if you come upon folks like Reggie, Les and the young boy with CP, ask what life is like for them. When you do this you are not only showing care and making that person feel like a valued human being, you also might be modeling for others. We're scared and curious about the unknown and that's okay. Just ask.

If you'd like to learn more about about Reggie and others who live with NF visit www.reggiebibbs.com.

The Science
of Anger

I was asked to help out with Gilda's Club, a charity organization that was started by Gilda Radner, one of the first actors in the famous improv group, Second City, in Chicago and one of the first cast members of *Saturday Night Live*. Gilda's Club helps individuals and families who are dealing with cancer and other serious illnesses. It assists them in dealing with treatment, handling recovery, and coping with the unfortunate occurrence of the death of a family member. The inspiration for Gilda's Club came from Radner's own battle with ovarian cancer. When she was dealing with her cancer, she found that being with other people helped everyone to either laugh about it or cry about it, and most importantly that they weren't alone. She found that there was so much healing power in the support of being physically surrounded and having social connections with other people that she wanted to start an organization that offered that kind of support. When she was struggling with her illness she said that she wanted to 'get her laugh back,' if nothing else for the healing powers that laughter brings.

The event that I was asked to participate in was called "Grief Night," which is a regular part of the local Gilda's Club weekly program. The people who asked me to volunteer made sure to tell me not to be afraid of using the words "death" and "dying." They don't use the typical phrases of someone "passed away" or "is no longer with us." They don't want to sugar coat death, even for kids, because it's not a sugary thing that they're going through. Instead you say something like, "I heard your mom died." They believe that it's important for people to call it what it is. The program that I hosted was particularly geared towards children who had a family member that died as a result of an illness. The instructions I was given were both specific and vague: I was told to dress up as a scientist and to make my character funny. After giving some thought to how I was going to integrate these two concepts, I put on a white lab coat, hung lab goggles around my neck, and adopted an exaggerated French accent, because let's face it, speaking bad French is always funny.

This Grief Night was specifically designed to address anger. Some of these children were filled with anger over what had happened to them, and this night was a way for them to express some of that anger and have fun at the same time.

I came out and introduced myself as "Doctor Pierre..." (insert indecipherable fake French gibberish). I started with a science experiment and called up a few kids to be my lab assistants in front of our group. We poured vinegar, baking soda, hydrogen peroxide, and food coloring into a large beaker, causing the multi-colored foam to overflow in a simulated volcanic eruption. Still in character, I explained the analogy that this experiment represented. In the activity we add little ingredients which represent little things that make us angry. Just like the ingredients, those little annoyances mix together inside of us and eventually they erupt, flowing out of us in a variety of ways. As I poured the ingredients in one by one, I asked the kids, "What are some things that people do that make us angry?"

They said things like, "When people get mad at us."

"When people call us names."

"When people hit us."

"When people tease us."

"Ok," I said, pouring in some vinegar or food coloring with each instance they provided. "So people do these things and that makes us angry. What else?"

Then one little girl said, "When people die."

"Ah, yes," I replied. "When this happens we get *very* angry," and I poured in some baking powder.

Eventually the mixture of ingredients reacted violently to one another and erupted from the beakers.

I asked the kids, "Now, what are some of the things you do when you turn into a volcano, when you get angry and erupt?" They volunteered different answers. They said things like, "We get mad, hit someone, yell at them, swear, cry, run away and be alone, not talk to anyone." All of us adults were taken aback by how many of the kids responded with graphic, violent answers. Hitting someone in the head. Punching them in the face. Kicking them in the stomach. We didn't try to correct this, though. We didn't say, "Well, that's a bad thing to do, a bad way to deal with your anger." We were careful not to deny their feelings. Working with kids like this it's important to understand that this is their way of expressing their emotions: to deal with it and to get it out. That's why we were there...that was the point of what we were doing.

The next science experiment I used as Dr. Pierre, was to have the kids balance a wooden dowel on the palm of their hands. As you would expect, it's difficult to keep the dowel stable and eventually it drops to the floor. The rule is that you have to keep trying no matter how many times you drop the stick. At one point, a young girl lost her balance for the third time, causing the stick to drop to the ground. She sighed deeply, and said in an exasperated tone of voice, "I have to pick this up, *again?*"

Her response went right to the heart of what this activity represents. When I finally stopped the exercise I asked the group, "What is the stick? What does it represent?" A five year old volunteered, "It's like life. Sometimes you have to balance it." We were all surprised that he hit the nail on the head on his first try. That's when I turned to the girl who was frustrated that she had to keep going with the exercise after dropping the stick many times. I pointed at her and asked, "Do you remember what you said? You said, 'I have to pick this up *again?*'"

"I did?"

"Yes, you did," I said, "and that's exactly what you have to do with life. When it feels out of control, when life falls apart, you have to pick it up again. But that's part of why we're all here tonight. You have to pick it up and keep going, but you don't have to do it alone."

At the end of the night, all of the volunteers and counselors came together to discuss what had occurred in that evening's Grief Night. With the kids gone, the social workers who work with these children on a regular basis informed me that there was one little boy who had expressed a special interest in me. I had an idea of who it was. The boy I was thinking of had been very outspoken about his violent feelings. During the stick exercise he was more interested in turning it into a sword than in getting it to balance on his hand. When the exercises were over, I put away my costume and was speaking in my normal voice when he said, "Hey, where did your accent go?" I told him that I'd put it in the car.

"Do you want another one? How about a pirate?" He nodded his head and I growled out, "Arrrrggg, matey. Walk the plank." He laughed.

The counselors revealed to me that this boy was an especially troubled child who was having a lot of behavior issues at school. He acted out his emotions in negative ways, wreaking havoc on his classroom. That night he was interested in who I was, and what I do. "Who is that guy?" he had asked the social workers. "What does he really do?" I think his confusion came from the fact that I was pretending to be a scientist, and I was funny and entertaining, as well as serious in talking about life and what it means. It was the combination of all of those things that sparked his curiosity.

My hunch is that this experience started to make him think that there was another way of being than just "the bad kid" or "the wild kid." There's another way to go through life than being constantly troubled or being in trouble. It's because he's hurting that he acts out in destructive ways; he wants attention and will do almost anything to get it. I can understand a little bit of what he's feeling. When I was young and hurting I acted out in ways that isolated me. I didn't know that there was another way to express myself, a way that would make people happy, even make them like me, make them laugh and cause them to think. This little boy is doing the same thing. He's just trying to fill a void. During that night at Gilda's Club I was getting all the attention, but instead of getting in trouble for it, people were laughing. But there were also quiet times during the evening, introspective moments, soulful moments. My gut tells me that these thoughtful times caught him off guard more than anything. He found himself under the spell of the games, the exercises, the laughter, and especially listening quietly to a story along with everyone else.

In fairy tales, folk tales, and legends, a character or characters, whether they're human or animals, are caught in a dilemma. They find themselves in tough, scary situations just like these kids—facing fears, demons, and overcoming challenges. In our lives we don't face the dangers of fairy tales, such as wicked witches or a pack of wolves, unless your mother-in-law is a teacher at Harry Potter's school. We face death, sickness, financial woes, and the breakdown of relationships. And these tests can be just as scary.

Through telling stories everyone in the audience gets to put themselves in the shoes of the protagonist. We become them. We think, "What would I do in that situation? How would I respond?" There are very quiet moments, somewhat tense and suspenseful when we are caught up in a story. We don't know what the outcome will be and that uncertainty freezes us in the moment. We're not released from that tension until the conflict is resolved. Once the conflict is overcome we are able to breathe a sigh of relief because we know that the character will live on, or not, but either way there's a resolution. Just like in real life until you face that fear, that bill that you have to pay, or that difficult conversation with a loved one, you'll continue to be frozen in that state.

As with folk tales, the exercises that I did with the kids were analogies aimed at both entertaining and instructing. They represent the difficult times in life and demonstrate that there is a way of surviving them.

Like balancing the stick, the more we move, walk around the room and sway with the stick's movements, the easier it is to keep it balanced upright. In life we do our best to respond to what the universe throws at us, and when we inevitably drop the stick, we pick it back up, and try again.

Body Parts

I was doing a workshop with a group of leadership students at a high school. These are the kids who are National Honors Society members, class presidents, tend to get good grades, and are peer-to-peer mediators. The students were standing in a line preparing to play a theater game that requires everyone to be at the ready, so when I call out someone's number that person has to step forward, salute me, and say a phrase. We were about ready to start when somebody asked a question about the game. Sarcastically I said, "Well, you all have your body parts as far as I can see, and that's all you really need for this, sooo..." A young lady stepped forward out of line, pulled off her prosthetic arm, saying, "We don't all have our real body parts." I was the only one in the room who didn't know this little hidden fact. They laughed at my shock.

After a long pause of embarrassment I said, "Okay, I stand corrected. Almost all of us have our real body parts. Now let's play the game with the body parts we do have." Everybody laughed, this time with me instead of at me. It ended up being a great workshop.

I love moments like this when I'm working with students,

because in that flash of embarrassment, the students are in the power seat. They all know something I don't. They get to be in control for a moment. They get to watch me learn, and usually the teachable moment has to do with humility. I try to own the moment, let them see me be the fool, and show them that when embarrassing moments strike us, you can get through it. I let them see me be vulnerable. I model the possibility of being wrong, not getting it, and still living through it.

In a slightly different way, as a parent, I've had to endure this with my own children. I've overreacted, yelled at them, and I was wrong. I've had to go back to my children, apologize, and admit that I shouldn't have reacted the way I did. It's very humbling to ask forgiveness from your own child.

As the speaker, the sage, the all-knowing dude who stands in front of an audience bestowing his wisdom, I've felt compelled to share a few of my humbling moments with audiences as well. It's strange to step out of the expected role of guru and instead reveal instances that bring to light just how much I don't know and still have to learn.

One time at a breakfast fundraiser for the United Way with 700 movers and shakers, I called a guy up on stage for an exercise. He just happened to being wearing a uniform that I thought I recognized. I asked the man, "Are you with the Salvation Army?"

The audience froze, dead quiet in the room. He said, "No. I'm a General with the United States Air Force." I paused in shame and said, "Oh crap! Are you going to find out where I live and drop a laser-guided bomb on my house now?"

"I'm thinking about it," he responded. Instantly, the whole room went crazy with laughter.

I just owned the moment, the blundering mistake. We all had a huge laugh at my expense, but it didn't matter. The relief came from us all knowing that we've all gotten it wrong before. They were just glad it was me and not them this time. When we slip up, it can be so humiliating and yet so funny at the same time, if we allow ourselves to own it. You see talk show hosts like Johnny Carson and David Letterman do this all the time. A joke flops, and they admit it was a train wreck, which often brings an even bigger laugh than the original joke.

Another eye-opening moment occurred after I finished speaking to a group of a few hundred National Guard members and their families. This instance wasn't so much funny or embarrassing as it was simply humbling.

A guy walked up to me and said, "That was a really good speech. I sometimes do what you do."

"Oh? Who do you speak to?" I asked.

"I talk to wounded soldiers and sometimes their wives."

I had noticed that while this man approached me he had a slight limp. I put the two thoughts together and asked if he was a wounded soldier himself.

"Yes sir," he answered. "I was the first casualty in '03 when we invaded Iraq." He then grabbed his slacks with both hands, just above his knees, and pulled them up to expose two metal shafts going into his shoes. He continued, "I had both legs blown off by an RPG."

In that moment I felt so overwhelmed by what he had gone through, what he's still living with, and the fact that he walked up to me with two prosthetic legs to thank me for my speech. I was fascinated with this man and humbled by what he apparently had suffered. I quickly turned the conversation to him, his life now, and more about his talks with other wounded soldiers.

At the time it had been six years since he'd lost his legs. He told me that the first two years were the hardest, but still every year at times he mourns his loss. He now has five kids, a wife, and friends that keep him moving and striving to make a difference in other wounded soldiers' lives.

He shared with me that his biggest claim to fame thus far was a talk he started doing that was apparently so groundbreaking that the Pentagon took action to evaluate it. It started when, while preparing to speak to a group of wounded soldiers and their wives, he realized that he didn't quite know what to say to the women. He turned to his wife for advice, and they decided to talk about sex after being wounded. This is what caused the stir with the top brass.

He told me that when they brought up this topic with the group the room got very quiet and not a single hand went up to ask a question. However, as soon as the talk was over the men surrounded him, and the women surrounded his wife. There were all kinds of questions that needed attending to for both genders.

He shared with me that it's common for soldiers who have lost a body part to feel as though they're not whole anymore. He explained that because of this they no longer feel sexually desirable. That way of thinking kills a lot of relationships, so he and his wife decided to broach the subject. They shared their personal experiences, encouraging others to talk about the issue out loud and face this scary and taboo topic that is so important to the strength and intimacy of a relationship.

We talk about soldiers, especially the wounded, as being heroes and warriors. But really, despite the bravery, they are human and are usually left with confusing emotions and complex problems when they return from combat.

What's so fascinating about this guy is that he didn't go home and crawl in a hole. He had his struggles to transition back into home life, but he took the time to process his experience, eventually taking the initiative to use this perspective from his pain and loss to help others.

Any time I speak to an audience I'm aware that there's a lot of life going on. I'm conscious of the fact that there are things I don't know about that are affecting their lives at that moment. Just like I couldn't see that the wounded veteran had lost his legs or that the high school girl didn't have a real arm, I don't know the personal experiences of the people to whom I'm speaking. Maybe someone is having an affair. Maybe someone else is going through a divorce. Perhaps someone recently experienced a death in the family. Often people are dealing with a sudden health issue for themselves or someone they love. I have to constantly be prepared for all of this to be present in the room. Not knowing any of it, I lay out a smorgasbord of ideas for people, and the audience walks up to the proverbial buffet and plates up what they need. Often people approach me after the talk and share that what they took away from it was just what they needed. It's a never ending reminder that people just need to hear certain things at certain times to reaffirm that what they're thinking and feeling is right.

As a speaker I don't share any story or idea with an audience that I don't find moving and meaningful myself. I don't have all the answers, but I find pieces and parts of answers through people's stories that I encounter along the way. The ones that I'm drawn to tend to be raw and filled with humility and honesty.

Being humbled isn't always a very fun experience, but it can help to keep us true to who we really are.

VI.
OPENING YOUR SOUL TO THE WORLD

Worried to Death

After hearing someone speak to an audience, have you ever been so moved by what they said that you wanted to talk with them afterward? Sometimes it's just an overwhelming need to engage with that speaker, or to share your gratitude for the talk. Sometimes it's just checking in with the speaker to share a personal discovery prompted by something they said...sort of a celebration of growth. It can also be a confirmation that what you heard said is really what they meant, you understood, you got it right. For me there's an urge to see if the speaker is for real. Are they as genuine in real life as they seemed when they were speaking on stage, or was it just an act? We all want the speaker to be sincere. We want a congruency between the person and the things they said. We want the outside to match what's on the inside. Otherwise it lessens what they say they believe. We want them to be real and not a hypocrite.

There's a little mistrust surrounding this because we've all been burned. How often do we encounter politicians and religious figures who have turned out to be the exact opposite of what they preach? Sometimes after I speak and a person comes up to me to connect, I feel a responsibility to live up to the ideas that I lay out for my audience. I've strived for an authenticity in my life. It's a challenge that I struggle with, to live up to all the ideas about life that I share with audiences.

Sometimes I wonder if what I've said has meant something to someone, to anyone. But there are those times when someone approaches me after the talk, and they wait around to be the last person, because what they want to talk about is usually very personal. They want the conversation to be private. I know when this happens, there's something I said that has connected with them. I never want to be that speaker who doesn't fulfill their wish to feel good about their discovery.

I perform a four minute story where I act out the life cycle from infancy to old age, all without saying a word. When people approach me about this they often cry. I usually just recognize their tears, let them cry, or listen. Sometimes that's the best way I can affirm that they got it right.

During a talk with 1st through 3rd graders who had difficulties with reading, I shared with them that when I was little I had a hard time learning to read. Immediately a little girl pointed at me and yelled out, "Just like me!" It was almost as though she was proud of it. She was so exited about the feeling of identifying with me, the feeling that she got it right.

Many times I have been asked to give a talk to students who are enrolled in Alternative Education programs, most of them grasping for their last chances at a high school diploma or GED. These schools are full of students with lots dysfunctions: broken families, multiple abuse issues, addiction, homelessness, gang affiliations... you get the idea. Many live with overwhelming pain in their lives. To relate to these students you have to touch on that level, go to that area of hurt. When speaking with students who have seen more tragedy than they should have to, I feel compelled to discuss issues of extreme hardship, sharing stories of my personal pain so that they can relate to me. That pain bonds us, and, I think, makes them feel that I'm not so different from them. Usually their reactions are silent, internal conversations with themselves. It's the same sentiment that the little girl so spontaneously and honestly expressed: "Just like me!"

After one such presentation to an Alternative Ed program of forty five students, a young man waited around to talk with me. When it was his turn, he walked respectfully up to me and stretched out his hand. I shook it. He said, "Thanks for your talk. The last thing you said really helped me."

"What was the last thing I said?" I asked, not remembering and needing to be honest.

"You told us about not worrying about death."

He's right. I told them a story about a time when I listened to a Buddhist priest at the University of California, Berkeley in Oakland. The conference focused on death and dying. The main speaker was Sogyal Rinpoche, author of the book, *The Tibetan Book of Living and Dying*. On a side note, a "Rinpoche" in the Buddhist faith means master or teacher. He's earned the right to teach and to write such a book.

At one point during his presentation, for whatever reason, he stopped talking, paused and said, "You know why you people in the West are so anxious about death?" The entire room suddenly got very quiet, very still. I sat up and came to the edge of my seat. I though to myself, "I *am* anxious about death. How did he know?" By the looks of the rest of the audience, it appeared we were all a bit preoccupied with this topic. Rinpoche said, "You are anxious about death, because death is like a train station, and you are waiting for the train to come, but your bags are not packed." He continued, "Your bags are the passions and dreams you have in your life that you have not done yet, and your bags are the people you love that you have not told. Pack bags. Train come." Had I not already been seated, I think I would have fallen down...the thought hit me that hard. It was a very shocking concept to suddenly hear.

At the time I was working in hospice. I had attended the conference hoping for insight into the common issues that arise when one reaches the end of *life*. I was at the conference to understand other peoples' deaths, not my own.

The young man who was now standing in front of me was very sincere. I could tell this story had hit him hard like it had me.

I asked, "What about this was meaningful to you?"

His eyes truly conveyed his tortured soul. I could see it was hard for him to hold back the tears.

He said, "I worry about death a lot. I worry about dying all the time, and I've heard that people who worry a lot about dying die sooner. So what you said really helped me."

So here's a young man standing in front of me that I have never met before, who, for whatever reason worries about dying. He understands the human psychology of anxiety and knows his body will be harmed if he continues to worry. He knows he is killing himself with worry, but can't stop doing it.

"What part of this story do you think has helped you?" I asked.

"I don't think I need to worry about dying so much. Maybe it's something else. Maybe there are other things in my life that I'm not doing, and that's really what I'm worried about...not doing what I really need to be doing."

We stood there for a few moments, just looking at each other, quietly letting this soulful moment take hold.

I finally said, "Yes, maybe think more about what it is you're not doing, not starting, not finishing, put more focus on that, and maybe the worry about death will move out of the way."

"I think so," he said.

We shook hands again; he smiled at me, and then turned and walked away, knowing he got it right!

~

I don't usually share my most intimate experience of death, which was the death of my sister in a car accident when I was 27. I hesitate to share this piece of my life with young people because chances are that most of them won't be able to relate to this kind of loss. I'm also cautious about sharing it because there could be kids in the audience who've had a family member die, like I did. It can get pretty emotional, which then can cause some embarrassment. I even go so far as to ask the principal before my talk if anyone has died recently. Often I'm glad I did because many times I'm informed that recently a student has died, and the pain is still fresh.

A month after this young man approached me, I told the story of my sister's death to students at a Christian high school. The focus of my talk was "spiritual moments," and something compelled me to share this painful experience. I wrapped up the talk by telling them that my first thought when I found out what had happened was, "My life has changed forever." The second thought I had was, "Did she know I loved her?" I suggested to the audience that at some point in their lives, they too will have to answer this question about someone close to them, someone they love.

After the talk, a young girl waited around to speak with me, just like the young man. Unlike the young man, however, she didn't want to tell me that she feared her own death. What she revealed was that she was plagued by a constant fear that her parents and brother were going to die. Every day when her family left for work or school she worried that something would happen to them, and they'd never come home again.

I asked her if she thought her fear had anything to do with the concept I had alluded to, that when we lose someone; we wonder if they knew we loved them. In other words, I wanted to know if the cause of her insecurity was the fact that she wasn't confident that her family members knew how much she cared for them.

This gave her pause. She gave me a sense that she had a hard time telling them how she felt. She had the urge to do something about this, but since she couldn't bring herself to share her feelings she took action in the form of worrying about them.

Again, it seems that this fear of death, whether for ourselves or for others, isn't so much about death as it is about life. For the young man, underlying this worry was a feeling that he wasn't doing what he should be doing in the present. For the young woman, the catalyst of her worry surrounding death came down to not communicating her feelings with her family. For both of them their worry was about something they weren't doing, but had control over. Therefore the worry over death consumed more and more of their time and energy.

When I heard Rinpoche speak, I expected that I would be learning about helping others to die gracefully and peacefully in my volunteer work with hospice. But when he asked, "Do you know why you in the West are so anxious about death?" I realized that I was and that I needed to explore that concept. When he gave the analogy of the train station, in my mind's eye I was standing at the train station. I had two bags, and they were both open with these clothes hanging out of them, some were even dirty. I knew the dirty clothes represented that I needed to clean up some relationships. Also, I realized I could get rid of some of clothes. I didn't need half the things hanging out of my bags, I didn't need to be carrying these unnecessary items. That visual was the beginning of understanding how to live in such a way that could help to avoid the uneasiness that comes with unfinished business. I will some-day be standing at that train station. Rinpoche ended by saying, "Pack bags, train come." He added, "Nobody has train schedule."

I was a young man at the time, and I realized that my relation-ship with death was directly related to how I was living life, right now. We don't know when death will visit us and we can't control it, but we can care for our relationships and be conscious of our actions. We can pack our bags. Only then will we be unafraid of the train's arrival.

Beginner's Mind: Act III

WONDERING OUT LOUD

This play recounts events as they truly occurred.

(A middle aged consultant named Tim is flying out of Grand Rapids, Michigan on his way to give a talk. A little girl is sitting right behind him, looking out the window and talking loudly to her dad as the plane starts to taxi.)

LITTLE GIRL

(loudly exclaims) I see another airplane!

DAD

Quiet, Honey. Yes, that's a plane.

LITTLE GIRL

Are we in the air yet?

DAD

No, we're still taxiing.

(The plane starts down the runway.)

LITTLE GIRL

Why are we going so fast?

DAD

We're going to take off soon.
(The plane takes off and begins to climb, quickly reaching hundreds of feet off the ground.)

LITTLE GIRL

I can see cars and buses.

DAD

I know.

LITTLE GIRL

I can see lots of things.
I can see all the way over there.
What are all these clouds?
We're higher than the clouds!
Can planes go higher than clouds?
When will we get there?

DAD

Soon, Honey.

Thoughts on "Wondering Out Loud"

The Little Girl's brilliance lies in her pure innocence, unadulterated honesty, and excitement for new discoveries.

The Little Girl, expressing her wonder and curiosity out loud, unfiltered, overflowing with questions about clouds, the plane, the wonderful phenomenon of taking flight, was so joyful. "Can planes fly higher than clouds?"

Yes. They can.

"Can I see more and further than I ever have before?"

Yes. You can.

If she had also asked her father, "If people are listening to me and hear my excitement about seeing something for the first time, could it remind them how fun it is to not know, to be in awe, to see the world with fresh eyes?"

Yes. It can.

Thank you, Little Girl.

THE END

Leaving a Memory

M y friend, Mary Jo, asked me to do a favor for her.
"Sure," I said, "What do you need?"

"I wondered if you would do a little storytelling show for these friends of mine. Their daughter, Sara, is homebound with an illness, and she really can't get out much. So, maybe you could go to her?"

I said, "How many people would be at their house?"

"Just Sara's Mom and Dad, her younger sister and me."

"Okay. You want me to perform a little show for five people in their living room?"

"Yes," she said.

"Alright, I'll do it."

This would be the smallest audience I'd ever performed for, and it was my first living room show. But, what the heck—a sick little girl! Maybe we could all have a few laughs, have some fun, and then I'd go home.

That's the visual I had in my head.

The day came to do my show. Mary Jo and I walk into the house. It's quiet. I meet Mom and Dad and the little sister. Dad then said, "I'll go get Sara." Minutes later I see Dad carrying Sara down the staircase. She's wearing a long flowery nightgown. Her head of hair is gone. She's bald, pale, and very thin.

I'm shocked. I didn't expect her to be this sick. I nudge Mary Jo and ask what's wrong with her. In a whisper she tells me, "Sara has cancer. They don't think she has much longer to live." I gave Mary Jo a look of, "You could have given me a little heads-up on the severity of the situation here."

My frame of mind has just made a huge shift. What I thought might be a festive, intimate event, just turned into a very sad feeling of helplessness. I thought, "What did I get myself into?" I felt so inept. How can I possibly make this a joyous occasion? How can my stories help her feel better?

Dad laid Sara on the sofa, her head propped up on pillows.

I open my show with a story called "The Leopard and Explorer." It's funny and a little scary. I change my voice into that of an island man, with a deep timbre and thick accent. Sara smiles and laughs through thirty minutes of storytelling. Eventually we say our goodbyes.

When we reached the privacy of the car, I told Mary Jo that I felt terrible, horrible. I was angry. It felt like what I'd done was completely meaningless. I didn't help her. I can't do a thing for this little girl. I can't save her. Mary Jo assured me that it was great. Sara had fun. The whole family laughed together. It was fine.

"No!" I said. "Why couldn't I be really smart and be a researcher or a scientist and come up with a cure for her? What I just did was nothing. I didn't change a thing. It was meaningless."

That feeling slowly receded, and the entire event became a faded memory.

Eight years later at Mary Jo's wedding reception, a couple walked up to me and said, "Hi, Tim! It's so good to see you. Do you remember us?"

"Ah, I'm sorry. I'm not sure. Can you give me a hint?"

"You came to our house and told stories to our daughter, Sara."

I was momentarily speechless, recalling the event that happened that day, and the fact that Sara had died a few weeks later. It all came back in that moment, how uncomfortable I was and how shameful I felt that I couldn't have done more for her.

I said, "Oh, yes. I remember. I'm sorry about Sara."

"Thanks." they say. "We just want you to know that we will ,never forget that you gave us some fond memories of Sara laughing and loving your stories. She talked about it for days later."

"Thank you," I said.

I'm not smart enough to be a researcher or scientist, but my feelings of inadequacy were misguided. Any time you can give someone a fond memory, a moment to recall in later years, you've done the best you can. I couldn't save her, but I was able to help create a memory.

There's a tendency in all of us at times to think that what we do in life or for work just doesn't matter. But *sometimes* we discover that it's in those moments in life where we think we didn't influence anything or anybody we made all the difference that needed to be made.

Personal Crest

I do an exercise during workshops where I have participants create a personal crest. On a blank sheet of paper I instruct them to draw five boxes to form the crest, and for each box there's a question. Instead of writing out the answer to each question, participants draw a picture of their answer in the designated box. There's something about drawing that forces people to visualize their answer in an image that lends itself to honest answers.

The five questions are:

What was a happy time in your life?

What was a sad time in your life?

What is a value that you're not willing to budge from?

What's something that you're proud of?

What is something you think is important you could tell others that would help them in their lives?

This exercise provides a unique way of looking at people. It puts them in a different light.

I've had a wide variety of responses to this exercise. Some people fall in love with the challenge of taking a look inside to answer the questions and make discoveries about themselves. Some folks are a little more cautious and ponder it for a minute or two, deciding if they're going to play along. Of course there are some skeptics who fold their arms across their chests and sit back in their chairs with blank looks of shock. They can't or won't even begin to go into this level of introspection. At times I think I've read facial expressions and body language of outright anger for even suggesting doing an exercise that could expose a glimpse of emotional vulnerability.

It's true that this exercise can be challenging, but it can also be extremely fulfilling if approached with honesty and an open mind. My first introduction to this exercise was as a family crest. My wife and two young kids had an hour to sit together and come to an agreement as a family on what we would choose to draw as a representation of our answers to each question. As a family or as an individual, making choices about what to draw causes one to really think about the answer to these questions. These answers will change as time goes on, because our lives are always changing.

Although we all have different lives, when you stop to think about it, there are so many experiences that we can relate to in one another. Sharing our stories is a powerful way of expressing who we are. It reveals that each human life has the magical quality of being both unique and the same as that of another.

Below is an example of a Personal Crest that I did while writing this book.

Tim's Personal Crest

Your Personal Crest

Create Your Own Crest

Afterword

A couple of *"Me Too"* stories occurred during the creation of this book.

The first story I'd say is a little poetic justice. In college my remedial English Class (English 101) was taught by Professor Ben Lockerd. At that time he was finishing his Ph. D. dissertation. When I discovered this little tidbit, I would tease him as I walked into class by saying in a French accent, "Ha, Monsieur Docteur Lockerd!" He corrected me with "Stop saying that. I'm not a doctor, yet."

Professor Lockerd obtained his Ph. D., but he never received any English papers from me. I told him, "You don't want to see what I wrote."

As fate would have it, thirty years later, his daughter, Marie Lockerd, became my editor, writer, helper, and now friend. This book would not be what it is without her brilliant writing skills, sensitivity, and allowing me to stay true to what I wanted to say without shame. My lack of writing skills, spelling ability and sentence structure was never an issue with her. Thank you, Marie.

P.S. Professor Lockerd, I'm sorry this paper is a little late. I did get help, but I'm finally handing it in.

~

The second happenstance occurred when I started looking for help with the layout and printing of the book. My wife put a listing on LinkedIn that I was looking for ideas on self-publishing. One of the responses came from a woman named Laura. I called her to ask about the next steps concerning obtaining an ISBN number, bar codes, layout, etc. She sounded up-beat and enthusiastic about my book—all this coming from someone I've never met before. I emotionally sensed that something was right about this. Her husband also owns a printing company. A few weeks later we met at her husband's printing company, Color House Graphics in Grand Rapids, MI. We sat down at a round table in Ken's office and proceed to chit chat, when suddenly Ken stopped everything and said, "I know you. You and I have met before."

"Really," I said, "When did we meet?" He said, "Year's ago at Ada Bible Church one Sunday. You were sitting next to me, and at that time I was going through a lot of painful things. You saw I was hurting. You put your hand on my shoulder and asked if I was all right. I lied and said I was fine. But I remember you from that moment."

This gave me pause as I sat back in my chair and thought, "Of all of the people who could help me publish this book, I chose Laura. Of all the printing companies in the world, I was led to this one—the one owned by the man who my gut, the spirit, moved me to touch one day at church." At that moment I knew where I was printing my book.

The End

ACKNOWLEDGEMENTS

Love and Gratitude to:

First and foremost, my wife, Anne Armstrong Cusack, who sat at the kitchen table and listened to every hand-written story. Without her encouragement, I would have stopped writing. Thank you for all your support. I love you. You can get new shoes now!

My kids, Isabel and Malcolm, for letting me tell others how they have changed my life.

The poet David Whyte whose poem, " Start Close In, " started me on my book journey.

Rob Bell who inspired me to create and to do more with what I have.

Ted Klontz who has told me for years," It's not on the outside—it's inside of you."

Dan Mosher who was one of the first people to say, "You should write a book."

Bob Moyer, my story theater professor, who gave me the feeling of coming home while I was in college.

My father, Patrick Quintin Cusack, and Mother, Agnes McGrath Cusack, for modeling how to be a good person, teaching me to be open, and showing me how to care for others.

My siblings: Gini, Kevin, Dan, Paul, Rosie, Rita, Ann, Ted and Marty—for helping to shape who I became...you did good, right?

Ty Sells, thank you for your honesty, creativity, and friendship.

Marcella Scott who was the first person to transcribe my stories from the yellow legal pads (no easy task) onto the typed page.

Molly Cusack for help with editing the cover design to get it exactly the way I wanted it.

Becky Ewing for giving me some of the first feedback that gave me comfort when I really needed it.

The men and women who have served our county in the military. I feel you should be thanked every day.

To order more copies of *Me Too* go to www.timcusack.com